THE INTERNATIONAL JEWISH COOK BOOK

By

FLORENCE KREISLER GREENBAUM

Instructor in Cooking and Domestic Science

RECIPES ACCORDING TO THE JEWISH DIETARY LAWS WITH *the* RULES *for* KASHERING

* * * * *

THE FAVORITE RECIPES OF AMERICA, AUSTRIA, GERMANY, RUSSIA, FRANCE, POLAND, ROUMANIA, Etc., Etc.

SECOND EDITION

PUBLISHERS' NOTE

It is with pleasure, and pardonable pride, that the Publishers announce the appearance of *The International Jewish Cook Book*, which, "though we do say it ourselves," is the best and most complete *kosher* cook book ever issued in this country. It is the direct successor to the "Aunt Babette Cook

Book," which has enjoyed undisputed popularity for more than a generation and which is no longer published. *The International Jewish Cook Book* is, however, far superior to the older book. It is much larger and the recipes are prepared strictly in accordance with the Jewish dietary laws.

The author and compiler, Mrs. Florence K. Greenbaum, is a household efficiency woman, an expert Jewish cook, and thoroughly understands the scientific combining of foods. She is a graduate of Hunter College of New York City, where she made a special study of diet and the chemistry of foods. She was Instructor in Cooking and Domestic Science in the Young Women's Hebrew Association of New York, and is now Instructor and Lecturer for the Association of Jewish Home Makers and the Central Jewish Institute, both under the auspices of the Bureau of Jewish Education (Kehillah).

Mrs. Greenbaum knows the housewife's problems through years of personal experience, and knows also how to economize. Many of these recipes have been used in her household for three generations and are still used daily in her home. There is no one better qualified to write a Jewish Cook Book than she.

Suggestions and additional recipes, for inclusion in later editions of the book, will be gratefully accepted by

THE PUBLISHERS. *NewYork,February ,*

PREFACE

In compiling these recipes every effort has been made to bear in mind the resources of the Jewish kitchen, as well as the need of being economical and practical.

The aim throughout has been to lay special emphasis on those dishes which are characteristically Jewish—those time-honored recipes which have been handed down the generations by Jewish housewives (for the Sabbath, Passover, etc). But the book contains a great many other recipes besides these, for the Jewish cook is glad to learn from her neighbors. Here will be found the favorite recipes of Germany, Hungary, Austria, France, Russia, Poland, Roumania, etc.; also hundreds of recipes used in the American household. In fact, the book contains recipes of every kind of food appealing to the Jewish taste, which the Jewish housewife has been able to adapt to the dietary laws, thus making the Cook Book truly *International*.

The manner of presentation is clear and simple, and if directions are followed carefully, will insure success to the inexperienced housewife. For the book has been largely planned to assist her in preparing wholesome, attractive meals; to serve the simplest as well as the most elaborate repast—from appetizer to dessert—without transgressing the dietary laws. At the same time the book offers many valuable suggestions and hints to the most expert cook.

In this book are also directions for making meat substitutes and many economies of the hour, which have been added to meet the needs of the present day.

REMARKS

The Jewish housewife enjoys the enviable reputation of being a good cook; in fact she is quite famous for her savory and varied dishes. Her skill is due not so much to a different method of cooking as to her ingenuity in combining food materials. The very cuts of meat she has been always accustomed to use, are those which modern cooks are now advising all to use. The use of vegetables with just enough meat to flavor, as for instance in the Shabbos Shalet, is now being highly recommended.

While it is not given to each and every woman to be a good cook, she can easily acquire some knowledge of the principles of cooking, namely:

1. That heat from coal, charcoal, wood, gas or electricity is used as a medium for toasting, broiling or roasting.

2. That heat from water is used as a medium for boiling, simmering, stewing or steaming.

3. That heat from fat is used as a medium for deep fat frying.

4. That heat from heated surfaces is used in pan-broiling, sauté, baking, braising or pot-roasting.

The length of time required to cook different articles varies with the size and weight of same—and here is where the judgment of the housewife counts. She must understand how to keep the fire at the proper temperature, and how to manage the range or stove.

In planning meals try to avoid monotony; do not have the same foods for the same days each week. Try new and unknown dishes by way of variety. Pay attention to garnishing, thereby making the dishes attractive to the eye as well as to the palate.

The recipes in this book are planned for a family of five, but in some instances desserts, puddings and vegetables may be used for two meals. Cakes are good for several days.

Do not consider the use of eggs, milk and cream an extravagance where required for certain desserts or sauces for vegetables, as their use adds to the actual food value of the dish.

As a rule the typical Jewish dish contains a large proportion of fat which when combined with cereal or vegetable fruits, nuts, sugar or honey, forms a dish supplying all the nourishment required for a well-balanced meal. Many of these dishes, when combined with meat, require but a small proportion of same.

Wherever fat is called for, it is intended that melted fat or dripping be used. In many of the dishes where fat is required for frying, any of the good vegetable oils or butter substitutes may be used equally well. These substitutes may also be used in place of butter or fat when same is required as an ingredient for the dish itself. In such cases less fat must be used, and more salt added. It is well to follow the directions given on the containers of such substitutes.

It is understood that all meats be made *kosher*.

RULES FOR KASHERING

In the religious and dietary laws of the Jewish people, the term "kasher" is applied to the preparation of meat and poultry, and means "to render fit" or "proper" for eating.

1. To render meat "fit" for food, the animal must be killed and cut up according to the Jewish method of slaughter, and must be purchased from a Jewish butcher.

2. The meat should be put into a pan, especially reserved for this purpose, entirely covered with cold water, and left to soak for half an hour. Before removing the meat from the water every particle of blood must be washed off. It should then be put upon the salting board (a smooth wooden board), placed in a slanting position, or upon a board with numerous perforations, in order to allow the blood to freely flow down. The meat should then be profusely sprinkled on all sides with salt, and allowed to remain in salt for one hour. It is then removed, held over a sink or pan, and well rinsed with cold water three times, so that all the salt is washed off. Meat left for three days or more unsoaked and unsalted, may be used only for broiling over coals; it may not be cooked in any other way.

The ends of the hoofs and the claws of poultry must be cut off before the feet are *kashered*.

Bones with no meat or fat adhering to them must be soaked separately, and during the salting should not be placed near the meat.

3. The liver must be prepared apart from the meat. It must be cut open in both directions, washed in cold water, and broiled over the fire, and salted while it is broiling. It should be seared on all sides. Water must then be poured over it, to wash the blood away. It may then be used in any manner, as the heat has drawn out the blood. Small steaks and chops may be *kashered* in the same way.

4. The heart must be cut open, lengthwise, and the tip removed before being soaked, so that the blood may flow out. The lungs likewise must be cut open before being soaked. Milt must have veins removed.

5. The head and feet may be *kashered* with the hair or skin adhering to them. The head should, however, be cut open, the brain taken out, and *kashered* separately.

6. To *kasher* suet or fat for clarifying, remove skin, and proceed as with meat.

7. Joints from hind-quarters must not be used, until they have been "porged," which means that all veins of blood, forbidden fat, and prohibited sinew have been removed. In New York City no hind-quarter meat is used by orthodox Jews.

8. All poultry must be drawn, and the inside removed before putting in water.

Cut the head off and cut the skin along the neck; find the vein which lies between the tendons, and trace it as far back as possible; at the back of the neck it divides into two branches, and these must be removed.

Cut off the tips of the wings and the claws of the feet. Proceed as with meat, first cutting open the heart and the liver. Eggs found inside of poultry, with or without shells, must be soaked and when salted be placed in such a position that the blood from the meat does not flow upon them. Such eggs may not be eaten with milk foods.

In conducting a kosher kitchen care must be taken not to mix meat and milk, or meat and butter at the same meal.

The utensils used in the cooking and serving of meat dishes may not be used for milk dishes. They should never be mixed.

Only soaps and scouring powders which contain no animal fat are permitted to be used in washing utensils. Kosher soap, made according to directions for making hard soap, may be used in washing meat dishes and utensils.

To follow the spirit as well as the letter of the dietary laws, scrupulous cleanliness should always be observed in the storing, handling and serving of food.

It is very necessary to keep the hands clean, the flours and cereals clean, the ice-box clean, and the pots and pans clean.

APPETIZERS

CANAPÉS

For serving at the beginning of dinner and giving a zest to the appetite, canapés are extremely useful. They may be either hot or cold and made of anything that can be utilized for a sandwich filling. The foundation bread should be two days old and may be toasted or fried crouton fashion. The nicest way is to butter it lightly, then set it in a hot oven to brown delicately, or fry in hot fat.

The bread should be cut oblong, diamond shaped, in rounds, or with a cutter that has a fluted edge. While the toast is quite hot, spread with the prepared mixture and serve on a small plate with sprigs of watercress or points of lemon as a garnish.

Another way is to cut the bread into delicate fingers, pile it log-cabin fashion, and garnish the centre with a stuffed olive. For cheese canapés sprinkle the toast thickly with grated cheese, well seasoned with salt and pepper. Set in a hot oven until the cheese melts and serve immediately.

SARDINE CANAPÉS

Toast lightly diamond-shaped slices of stale bread and spread with a sardine mixture made as follows:—Skin and bone six sardines, put them in a bowl and run to a paste with a silver spoon. Add two tablespoons of lemon juice, a few drops of Worcestershire sauce, a dash of pepper, two teaspoons of chopped parsley and four tablespoons of creamed butter. Garnish with a border of whites of hard-boiled eggs, finely chopped, and on top scatter shredded olives.

WHITE CAVIAR

Take roe of any fish, remove skin, salt; set aside over night. Next day beat roe apart, pour boiling water over it and stir; when roe is white, pour off the water and let drain; then put in pan with two tablespoons of oil and salt, pepper, a little vinegar, and mix well. Let stand a few days before using.

This caviar may be substituted in all recipes for the Russian caviar or domestic caviar may be procured in some shops.

CAVIAR CANAPÉS

Cut the bread about one-quarter of an inch thick and two inches square (or round), and after it is toasted spread over each slice a teaspoon of ice cold caviar. Mix one teaspoon of chopped onion and one teaspoon chopped parsley; spread the mixture over the caviar and serve with quarters of lemon.

ANCHOVY CANAPÉS

Cut the bread as for caviar canapés and spread with anchovy paste. Chop separately the yolks and whites of hard-boiled eggs and cover the canapés, dividing them into quarters, with anchovies split in two lengthwise, and using yolks and whites in alternate quarters.

ANCHOVY CANAPÉS WITH TOMATOES

For each person take a thin slice toast covered with anchovy paste. Upon this place whole egg which has been boiled four minutes, so that it can be pealed whole and the yolk is still soft. Around the toast put tomato sauce.

CHOPPED ONION AND CHICKEN FAT

Chop one yellow onion very fine, add four tablespoons of chicken fat (melted), salt to taste. Serve on slices of rye bread. If desired, a hard-boiled egg chopped very fine may be mixed with the onions.

BRAIN (APPETIZER)

Cook brains, let cool and add salt; beat up with chopped onions, juice of one and a half lemons and olive oil. Serve on lettuce leaves.

BLACK OLIVES

Pit black olives, cut them very thin, and prepare as brain appetizer; beat well with fork.

CHICKEN LIVER PASTE, No. 1

Wash thoroughly several fowls' livers and then let them simmer until tender in a little strong soup stock, adding some sliced mushroom, minced onion, and a little pepper and salt. When thoroughly done mince the whole finely, or pound it in a mortar. Now put it back in the saucepan and mix well with the yolks of sufficient eggs to make the whole fairly moist. Warm over the fire, stirring frequently until the mixture is quite thick, taking care that it does not burn.

It should be served upon rounds of toast on a hot dish garnished with parsley.

IMITATION PATE DE FOI GRAS

Take as many livers and gizzards of any kind of fowl as you may have on hand; add to these three tablespoons of chicken or goose fat, a finely chopped onion, one tablespoon of pungent sauce, and salt and white pepper to taste. Boil the livers until quite done and drain; when cold, rub to a smooth paste. Take some of the fat and chopped onion and simmer together slowly for ten minutes. Strain through a thin muslin bag, pressing the bag tightly, turn into a bowl and mix with the seasoning; work all together for a long time, then grease a bowl or cups and press this mixture into them; when soft cut up the gizzards into bits and lay between the mixture. You may season this highly, or to suit taste.

CHICKEN LIVER PASTE, No. 2

Take one-quarter pound chicken livers that have been boiled soft; drain and rub through grater, add one-quarter cup of fresh mushrooms that have been fried for three minutes in two tablespoons of chicken fat, chop these, mix smooth with the liver, moistening with the fat used in frying the mushrooms, season with salt, pepper, paprika and a little onion and lemon juice. Spread on rye bread slices. Garnish plate with a red radish or sprigs of parsley.

CHOPPED HERRING

Soak herring a few hours, when washed and cleaned, bone and chop. To one herring take one onion, one sour apple, a slice of white bread which has been soaked in vinegar, chop all these; add one teaspoon oil, a little cinnamon and pepper. Put on platter in shape of a herring with head at top and tail at bottom of dish, and sprinkle the chopped white of a hard-boiled egg over fish and then the chopped yolk.

CHEESE BALLS

Take mashed cream cheese—add butter, cream and a little paprika. You can chop either green peppers, almonds or olives in this mixture, or the juice of an onion. Roll into small balls and serve on lettuce leaves. This is also very good for sandwiches.

EGG APPETIZER

Boil eggs hard. Cut slice off the end, so that the egg will stand firm. Dip egg in French dressing, then with a pastry bag arrange sardellen butter on the top of egg. Have ready small squares of toasted bread, spread with a thin layer of sardellen butter, on which to stand the eggs. Caviar, mixed with some finely chopped onion, pepper and lemon juice, may be used instead of the sardellen butter, but mayonnaise must be used over the caviar.

DEVILED EGGS WITH HOT SAUCE

Take six hard-boiled eggs, cut lengthwise, remove yolk and add to same: one dessertspoon of melted butter, Cayenne pepper, salt and chopped parsley. Mash this mixture very fine and refill the whites of the eggs and turn over on platter.

Sauce.—One tablespoon of butter, one tablespoon of flour, a pinch of Cayenne pepper, salt and one pint of milk. Stir this mixture continually until it thickens; beat the yolk of one egg and pour the hot gravy over the same. Dress with chopped parsley and eat very hot. Sherry wine can be added if desired.

STUFFED YELLOW TOMATOES

Take small yellow tomatoes, scrape out the centre and fill with caviar. Serve on lettuce or watercress.

A DELICIOUS APPETIZER

Take as many slices of delicately browned toast as people to serve, several large, firm tomatoes sliced, one green pepper, and store cheese. Place a slice of tomato on each slice of toast and season with salt and pepper and a dot of butter. Place several long, curly strips of pepper around the tomato, and cover with a thin slice of the cheese. Place in the oven until the cheese is melted. Serve piping hot.

CELERY RELISH

Boil about six pieces of celery root. When soft, peel and mash. Season with salt, pepper, a little onion powder, a teaspoon of home-made mustard and plenty of mayonnaise. Shape into pyramids, put mayonnaise on the top of the pyramid, and on top of that either a little well-seasoned caviar or some sardellen butter shaped in a pastry bag. Serve on a slice of beets and a lettuce leaf.

SARDELLEN

Take one-quarter pound salted sardellen and soak in water over night. Bone the next morning, put in cloth and press until dry; chop very fine, almost to a paste; take one-half pound sweet butter, stir to a cream and add the sardellen. Serve on toasted cracker or bread. Sprinkle with the grated yellow and grated white of egg.

STUFFED EGGS

Hard boil eggs, drop into cold water, remove shells, cut each in half lengthwise. Turn out yolks into a bowl. Carefully place whites together in pairs, mash yolks with back of a spoon. For every six yolks put into bowl one tablespoon melted butter, one-half teaspoon mustard (the kind prepared for table), one teaspoon salt, dash of cayenne pepper. Rub these together thoroughly with yolks. Make little balls of this paste the size of the yolks. Fit one ball into each pair whites.

NUT AND CHEESE RELISH

Mix one package cream cheese with one cup of chopped nut meats, one teaspoon of chopped parsley, two tablespoons of whipped cream, salt and red pepper. Roll into balls and serve cold, garnished with parsley and chopped nuts.

GRAPE-FRUIT COCKTAIL

Cut the grape-fruit into halves, crosswise, and scoop out the pulp, rejecting the white inner skin as well as the seeds. Clean the shells; cut the edges with a sharp knife into scallops and throw them into cold water. Set the pulp on the ice. At serving time put a teaspoon of cracked ice in the bottom of each shell; fill with the pulp, mixed thoroughly with powdered sugar and a little sherry, if desired; and place a maraschino cherry or bit of bright-colored jelly in the centre of each. Lay on paper doilies or surround with bits of asparagus fern.

AMBROSIA

Fill glass with alternate layers of sliced orange and cocoanut; cover with powdered sugar and place a maraschino cherry on the top of each.

PEACH COCKTAIL

Fill the glasses with sliced peaches; cover with orange or lemon juice; sweeten to taste; add a little shaved ice and serve.

Apricot and cherry cocktails may be made in the same way.

RASPBERRY COCKTAIL

Mash a pint of ripe, red currants; strain them through cheesecloth; pour the juice over a pint of red raspberries and set on the ice to chill. At serving time sweeten to taste and pour into the glasses, putting one teaspoon of powdered sugar on the top of each.

PINEAPPLE AND BANANA COCKTAIL

Take equal parts of banana and fresh or canned pineapple; cut into small cubes and cover with lemon or pineapple juice. Serve in glasses or orange shells placed on autumn leaves or sprays of green fern.

STRAWBERRY COCKTAIL

Slice five or six large strawberries into each glass and squeeze over them the juice of an orange. At serving time add one heaping teaspoon of powdered sugar and one tablespoon of shaved ice.

MUSK MELONS

Cut melon in half, seed and put on ice one hour before serving. When ready to serve, fill with crushed ice and sprinkle with, powdered sugar. Allow one-half melon for each person. Very refreshing for summer luncheons or dinners. For dinner serve before soup.

FILLED LEMONS

Select good-sized lemons; cut off tip to stand the lemon upright; cut top for cover. Scoop out all the lemon pulp, and put in a bowl; put shells in a bowl of cold water. For six lemons take one box of boneless sardines, six anchovies, and two green peppers, cut very fine. Wet with lemon-juice until moist; fill in shells after wiping dry; insert a pimento on top; put on cover of lemon; serve on doily with horseradish and watercress.

RED PEPPER CANAPÉS

Mix together two chopped hard-boiled eggs, one tablespoon of chopped red peppers (canned), a saltspoon of salt, a tiny pinch of mustard and two tablespoons of grated American cheese with sufficient melted butter to form a paste; spread over the rounds of fried bread and place in a very hot oven for about three minutes. Serve on a folded napkin, garnished with watercress.

SALTED PEANUTS

Shell and skin freshly roasted peanuts and proceed as in salting almonds.

SALTED ALMONDS

Pour boiling water on the almonds; cool and remove the skins; dry thoroughly and brown in a hot oven, using a half tablespoon of butter or olive oil (preferably the oil) to each cup of nuts, which must be shaken frequently. When brown, sprinkle well with salt and spread on paper to dry and cool.

A still easier way to prepare the nuts is to cook them over the fire, using a larger quantity of olive oil. As the oil can be saved and used again, this method is not necessarily extravagant.

SANDWICHES

Bread should be twenty-four hours old and cut in thin, even slices. If fancy forms are desired, shape before spreading with butter. Cream butter and spread evenly.

ANCHOVY SANDWICHES

Pound the anchovies to a paste and mix with an equal quantity of olives stoned and finely chopped.

CELERY SANDWICHES

Two cups of chopped celery, two tablespoons of chopped walnuts, two tablespoons of chopped olives, quarter of a cup of Mayonnaise dressing. Spread between slices of thin buttered bread.

FISH SANDWICHES

Spread one piece of bread with any kind of cold fish that has been shredded and mixed with tartar sauce. Then put a lettuce leaf on that and then a slice of hard-boiled egg that has been dipped in tartar sauce. Cover with a slice of buttered bread.

NUT AND RAISIN SANDWICHES

Take equal quantities of nuts and raisins; moisten with cream or grape juice and spread on thin slices of bread.

BROWN BREAD SANDWICHES

Season one cup of cottage cheese with salt, cayenne, and add one pimento cut in shreds. Cut white and brown bread in finger lengths about one inch wide. Spread with cheese mixture and place a brown and white slice together.

CHEESE AND NUT SANDWICHES

Cut thin rounds from rye bread. Spread with the following mixture: take one cream cheese, rub to a cream, season to taste with salt and paprika, add one stalk of chopped celery, and one-fourth cup of chopped nut meats. Spread on buttered bread and place a slice of stuffed olive on top, in the centre of each piece of bread.

LETTUCE SANDWICHES

Put fresh lettuce leaves, washed and dried, between thin layers of bread. Spread with Mayonnaise or Boiled Dressing.

OLIVE SANDWICHES

Take either ripe or green olives; remove the seeds; mince and mix thoroughly with Mayonnaise dressing. Spread between slices of whole-wheat or graham bread.

SARDINE SANDWICHES

Remove the skin and bones from the sardines. Rub to a paste, adding an equal quantity of chopped hard-boiled eggs, seasoned with salt, cayenne, lemon juice or vinegar. Moisten with melted butter and spread between slices of bread.

DATE AND FIG SANDWICHES

Wash equal quantities of dates and figs; stone the dates; add blanched almonds in quantity about one-fourth of the entire bulk; then run the whole mixture through a food chopper. Moisten with orange juice and press tightly into baking-powder tins. When ready to use, dip the box in hot water; turn out the mixture; slice and place between thin slices of buttered bread.

FIG SANDWICHES

Remove the stems and chop the figs fine. Put in a double boiler with a little water and cook until a paste is formed. Add a few drops of lemon juice; set aside; when cool spread on thin slices of buttered bread.

EGG SANDWICHES

Hard boil the eggs, place them immediately into cold water. When cold; remove the shells carefully, cut the eggs in half lengthwise and butter slightly. Lay one or two sardellen or appetite silds on one half of the egg and press the one half gently on the other half which has the sardellen. The egg must appear whole. Now tie lengthwise and across with the narrowest, various colored ribbons you can find.

CHESTNUT SANDWICHES

One slice each of white and brown bread, cut thin and buttered, and spread with chestnuts that have been boiled tender, peeled and rubbed through a sieve, then mashed with hard-boiled eggs to a paste and moistened with Mayonnaise.

SALMON AND BROWN BREAD SANDWICHES

Flake one cup salmon and rub it to a paste. Add mustard, salt, and cayenne. Spread on the bread, cover with a layer of thin slices of cucumber, then another piece of bread, press lightly and arrange with sprigs of parsley on the platter.

WHITE AND BROWN BREAD SANDWICHES

If a novel sandwich is wanted, butter alternate slices of brown and white bread and pile them one above the other in a loaf. Cut the new loaf across the slices, butter them and pile them so that when this second loaf is cut, the slices will be in white and brown blocks. Press the slices very closely together before cutting at all.

TOASTED CHEESE SANDWICHES

The filling for the toasted cheese sandwiches calls for a cup of soft, mild cheese, finely cut, and stirred over the fire with a tablespoon of butter until the cheese is melted. Enough milk to moisten, perhaps not more than one-eighth of a cup, is then added, with salt, mustard, and paprika to taste, and the whole is stirred until creamy and smooth. Slices of bread are very thinly buttered, the cheese mixture spread on generously, each slice covered with another slice, and set away until the filling cools and hardens, when the sandwiches are toasted on both sides and served hot.

POACHED EGG SANDWICHES

Slice as many pieces of bread, from a round loaf, as you have persons to serve. Toast these slices and let cool. Across each slice place three strips of pimentoes (use the canned pimentoes), on top of that place a cold poached egg, put a teaspoon of Mayonnaise on the top of the egg and sprigs of watercress encircling the toast.

MUSTARD SARDINE PASTE FOR SANDWICHES

Take one box of mustard sardines; bone and mash; add to the mixture one tablespoon of tomato catsup, one teaspoon of Worcestershire sauce, juice of one lemon, a pinch of cayenne pepper, as much white pepper as will cover the end of a knife, two tablespoons of vinegar, and one tablespoon of olive oil. Mix thoroughly until it becomes a paste. Then spread on thinly cut bread for sandwiches.

CAVIAR AND SALMON SANDWICHES

Take a piece of rye bread, cut round (with a biscuit cutter), spread with mustard; put some caviar in centre of the bread, strips of smoked salmon around the caviar and strips of pickle around the salmon.

RIBBON SANDWICHES

Cut two, slices of white bread and two of brown. Butter three and spread with a thick paste made of hard-boiled egg very finely chopped and mixed with mayonnaise dressing. Build the slices up one above the other, alternating brown and white, and placing the unbuttered slice on top. Before serving, slice down as you would a layer cake.

EGG AND OLIVE SANDWICHES

Chop four eggs which have been boiled fifteen minutes, add two tablespoons of chopped olives, season and moisten with olive oil and vinegar. Spread between thin slices of buttered bread.

RUSSIAN SANDWICHES

Spread bread with thin slices of Neufchatel cheese, cover with finely chopped olives moistened with mayonnaise dressing.

SURPRISE SANDWICHES

Take orange marmalade, pecan nuts and cream cheese in equal quantities and after mixing thoroughly spread on thin slices of buttered bread.

CHICKEN SANDWICHES

Mince some cold roast or boiled chicken in a chopping bowl, then mix the gravy with it, adding a few hard-boiled eggs, which have been minced to a powder. Mix all into a soft paste. Then cut thin slices of bread, spread the chicken between the slices (if desired you may add a little mustard); press the pieces gently together.

CHICKEN SANDWICHES WITH MAYONNAISE

Grind up chicken in meat chopper. To each cup of chicken add one tablespoon of mayonnaise, and one tablespoon of chicken soup. Mix into soft paste, and put in finger-rolls.

DEVILED TONGUE SANDWICHES

Grind up tongue (root will do) in meat chopper; to a cup of ground tongue add one teaspoon of mustard, one tablespoon of soup, and one teaspoon of mayonnaise. Mix into soft paste; spread on white bread cut very thin.

MINCED GOOSE SANDWICHES

Take either boiled or roast goose (which has been highly seasoned) and mince in a chopping bowl, add one or two pickles, according to quantity, or a teaspoon of catsup. Spread thin slices of bread or nice fresh rolls, with a thin coating of goose oil, slightly salted, then spread the minced goose and cover with a layer of bread which has been previously spread.

VEAL SANDWICHES

May be prepared as above, or slice the veal in thin slices and spread with mustard.

BOILED, SMOKED, OR PICKLED TONGUE SANDWICHES

Remove the crust from the bread (unless it is very soft), place the slices of tongue (cut very thin) and lettuce leaves between the slices.

SOUPS

Soups are wholesome and palatable and should form part of the meal whenever possible. It is a good plan to have some sort of vegetable or meat stock always at hand, as this renders the making of the soup both easy and economical. With milk at hand, cream soups are easily made.

SOUP STOCK

In making soup, bring the cold water in the soup pot with the meat and bones to a boil slowly, and let it simmer for hours, never boiling and never ceasing to simmer. If clear soup is not desired soup may be allowed to boil. Bones, both fresh and those partly cooked, meats of all kinds, vegetables of various sorts, all may be added to the stock pot, to give flavor and nutriment to the soup.

One quart of cold water is used to each pound of meat for soup; to four quarts of water, one each of vegetables of medium size and a bouquet.

Make the soup in a closely covered kettle used for no other purpose. Remove scum when it first appears; after soup has simmered for four or five hours add vegetables and a bouquet.

Parsley wrapped around peppercorn, bayleaf, six cloves and other herbs, excepting sage, and tied, makes what is called a bouquet and may be easily removed from the soup.

Root celery, parsley, onions, carrots, asparagus and potatoes are the best vegetables to add to the soup stock. Never use celery leaves for beef soup. You may use celery leaves in potato soup, but sparingly, with chopped parsley leaves.

Vegetables, spices and salt should always be added the last hour of cooking. Strain into an earthen bowl and let cool uncovered, by so doing stock is less apt to ferment.

A cake of fat forms on the stock when cold, which excludes air and should not be removed until stock is used. To remove fat run a knife around edge of bowl and carefully remove the same. A small quantity will remain, which should be removed by passing a cloth, wrung out of hot water, around edge and over top of stock. This fat should be clarified and used for drippings. If time cannot be allowed for stock to cool before using, take off as much fat as possible with a spoon, and remove the remainder by passing tissue or any absorbent paper over the surface.

Bouillon should always be thickened with *yolks* of eggs, beat up with a spoon of cold water. Ordinary beef soup or tomato soup may be thickened with flour. To do this properly heat a scant spoon of soup drippings, stir in briskly a spoon of flour, and add gradually a large quantity of soup to prevent it becoming lumpy.

WHITE STOCK

Veal, turkey, chicken and fish are used.

BROWN STOCK

Follow directions given for bouillon, adding a slice of beef and browning some of the meat in the marrow from the bone.

BEET SOUP—RUSSIAN STYLE (FLEISCHIG)

Cut one large beet and one-half pound of onion in thick pieces and put in kettle with one pound of fat brisket of beef; cover with water and let cook slowly two hours; add three-fourths of a cup of sugar and a little citric acid to make it sweet and sour and let cook another hour; season and serve hot.

BORSHT

Take some red beetroots, wash thoroughly and peel, and then boil in a moderate quantity of water from two to three hours over a slow fire, by which time a strong red liquor should have been obtained. Strain off the liquor, adding lemon juice, sugar, and salt to taste, and when it has cooled a little, stir in sufficient yolks of eggs to slightly thicken it. May be used either cold or hot. In the latter case a little home-made beef stock may be added to the beet soup.

If after straining off the soup the remaining beetroot is not too much boiled away, it may be chopped fine with a little onion, vinegar and dripping, flavored with pepper and salt, and used as a vegetable.

SCHALET OR TSCHOLNT (SHABBAS SOUP)

Wash one pint of white haricot beans and one pint of coarse barley and put them into a covered pot or pan with some pieces of fat meat and some pieces of marrow bone, or the backs of two fat geese which have been skinned and well spiced with ginger and garlic. Season with pepper and salt and add sufficient water to cover. Cover the pot up tightly. If one has a coal range it can be placed in the oven on Friday afternoon and let remain there until Saturday noon. The heat of the oven will be sufficient to bake the Schalet if there was a nice clear fire when the porridge was put in the oven. If this dish cannot be baked at home it may be sent to a neighboring baker to be placed in the oven there to remain until Saturday noon, when it is called for. This takes the place of soup for the Sabbath dinner.

BOUILLON

Put on one three-pound chicken to boil in six quarts cold water. Take one and one-half or two pounds of beef and the same quantity thick part of veal, put in a baking-pan, set in the stove and brown quickly with just enough water to keep from burning. When brown, cut the meat in pieces, add this with all the juice it has drawn, to the chicken soup. Set on the back of the stove, and cook slowly all day. Set in a cold place, or on ice over night, and next morning after it is congealed, skim off every particle of fat.

Melt and season to taste when ready to serve. Excellent for the sick. When used for the table, cut up carrots and French peas already cooked can be added while heating.

If cooked on gas stove, cook over the simmering flame the same number of hours.

CONSOMMÉ

Take three pounds of beef, cut in dice and cover with three quarts of cold water. Simmer slowly for four hours. The last hour add one-half cup each of carrots, celery, onion, and season with one-half teaspoon of peppercorns and one tablespoon of salt. Strain, cool, remove fat and clear (allowing one egg-shell broken fine and the slightly beaten white of one egg to each quart of stock). Add to the stock, stir constantly until it has reached the boiling point. Boil two minutes and serve.

CHICKEN SOUP, No. 1

Take one large chicken, cook with four quarts of water for two or three hours. Skim carefully, when it begins to boil add parsley root, an onion, some asparagus, cut into bits. Season with salt, strain and beat up the yolk of an egg with one tablespoon of cold water, add to soup just before serving. This soup should not be too thin. Rice, barley, noodles or dumplings may be added. Make use of the chicken, either for salad or stew.

CHICKEN SOUP, No. 2

Take the carcass of a cold, cooked chicken and break into small pieces. Add one-half cup of chopped celery and one onion chopped fine. Cover with cold water; simmer slowly for two hours. Strain, add salt and pepper to taste.

CHICKEN BROTH

Cut the chicken into small pieces and place it in a deep earthen dish; add one quart of water; cover it and set over a kettle of boiling water, letting it steam until the meat of the chicken has become very tender. Strain off the broth and let it stand over night. In the morning remove the fat and return the liquid to the original earthen dish.

JULIENNE SOUP

Have soup stock ready. Boil in water until tender one cup green peas, three carrots cut up in small pieces, and some cabbage chopped fine. Brown two tablespoons of flour in a skillet in hot fat, then stir in the vegetables. Fry some livers and gizzards of fowls, if handy, and add, then stir in the strained soup stock.

RICE BROTH

May be made either of beef or mutton, adding all kinds of vegetables. Boil one-half cup of rice separately in a farina kettle. Strain the beef or mutton broth. Add the rice and boil one-half hour longer, with potatoes, cut into dice shape; use about two potatoes; then add the beaten yolk of an egg. Strained stock of chicken broth added to this soup makes it very palatable and nutritious for the sick.

MOCK TURTLE SOUP

Take one calf's head, wash well; put on to boil with four and one-half quarts of water; add two red peppers, onions, celery, carrots, cloves, salt to taste, and a little cabbage; boil six hours; also, have ready some meat stock; the next day put fat in a skillet with two large tablespoons of flour; let it brown; then, take the calf's head and cut all the meat from it in pieces; add the calf's tongue, cut in dice. Slice hard-boiled eggs, one glass of sherry; and one lemon sliced; put all in the stock; allow it to come just to a boil.

MUTTON BROTH

Cut three pounds of neck of lamb or lean shoulder into small pieces; cover closely and boil with three quarts of water, slowly, for two hours; add two tablespoons well-washed rice to the boiling soup. Cook an hour longer, slowly; watch carefully and stir from time to time. Strain and thicken it with a little flour; salt and pepper to taste. Particularly nice for invalids.

MULLIGATAWNY SOUP

Add to three quarts of liquor, in which fowls have been boiled, the following vegetables: three onions, two carrots, and one head of celery cut in small dice. Keep the kettle over a high heat until soup reaches the boiling point; then place where it will simmer for twenty-five minutes. Add one tablespoon of curry powder, one tablespoon of flour mixed together; add to the hot soup and cook five minutes. Pass through a sieve. Serve with small pieces of chicken or veal cut in it.

FARINA SOUP

When the soup stock has been strained and every particle of fat removed, return it to the kettle to boil. When it boils hard stir in carefully quarter of a cup of farina, do this slowly to prevent the farina from forming lumps. Stir into the soup bowl the yolk of one egg, add a teaspoon of cold water. Pour the soup into the bowl gradually and stir constantly until all has been poured into the bowl. Serve at once.

GREEN KERN SOUP

Soak one-half cup of green kern in a bowl of water over night. Put on two pounds of soup meat, add a carrot, an onion, a stalk of celery, a sprig of parsley, one or two tomatoes, a potato, in fact any vegetable you may happen to have at hand. Cover up closely and let it boil slowly over a low heat three or four hours. Put the green kern on to boil in water slightly salted, as it boils down keep adding soup stock from the kettle of soup on the stove, always straining through a hair sieve, until all has been used. Serve as it is or strain through a colander and put pieces of toasted bread into the soup.

Another way of using the green kern is to grind it to a powder.

NOODLE SOUP

For six persons, select a piece of meat off the neck, about two and one-half pounds; add three quarts of water, an onion, one celery root, two carrots, a large potato, some parsley, three tomatoes and the giblets of poultry. Cook in a closely covered kettle, letting the soup simmer for four or five hours. Remove every bit of scum that rises. Strain; add salt and remove every particle of fat; put in noodles; boil about five minutes and serve at once. If allowed to stand it will become thick.

MUSHROOM AND BARLEY SOUP

Take one quart of hot bouillon, add a quarter pound barley which has been boiled in water; and one ounce of dried mushrooms which have been thoroughly washed and cut in pieces, an onion, carrot, bayleaf, parsley and dill. Boil all these and when the vegetables are nearly tender, remove from soup, add the meat from the bouillon, cut up in small pieces, let soup come to a boil and serve.

OXTAIL SOUP

Wash two large oxtails and cut into pieces. Cut one onion fine and fry in one tablespoon of drippings. When brown, add oxtails to brown, then put into soup kettle with four quarts cold water. Add one tablespoon of salt, one tablespoon of mixed herbs, four cloves, four peppercorns. Simmer for three or four hours. Skim off fat, strain. Vegetables cut into fancy shapes and boiled twenty minutes may be added.

GREEN PEA SOUP

Make your soup stock as usual, adding a pint of washed pea-pods to the soup. Heat a tablespoon of drippings, put in the peas, with a little chopped parsley, cover closely and let simmer; keep adding soup stock when dry. When the peas are tender put into the strained soup. Season with one teaspoon of salt and two teaspoons of sugar, add drop dumplings to this soup before serving.

PIGEON SOUP

Make a beef soup, and an hour before wanted add a pigeon. Boil slowly, with all kinds of vegetables, provided your patient is allowed to have them. Strain, add the beaten yolk of an egg, salt to taste.

TURKEY SOUP

Cut up any bones or meat of cold turkey, and cook like soup made of left-over chicken and chicken bones.

OKRA GUMBO SOUP (SOUTHERN)

Take one quart of ripe tomatoes, stew with one quart of okra, cut into small rings. Put this on to boil with about two quarts or water and a piece of soup meat (no bone), chop up an onion, a carrot and a sprig of parsley, add this to the soup. Fricassee one chicken with some rice, dish up with the soup, putting a piece of chicken and one tablespoon of rice into each soup plate before adding the soup. Let the soup simmer four or five hours; season with salt and pepper. A little corn and Lima beans may be added; they should be cooked with the soup for several hours. Cut the soup meat into small cubes and leave in the soup to serve.

TCHORBA—TURKISH SOUP

Take one pound of meat, cover with water and boil till meat is tender. Boil rice in another pan until it is creamy, when ready to serve, add one beaten egg and juice of half a lemon.

Broken rice is best for this dish.

BARLEY SOUP

Take one cup of barley, two onions cut fine, one-half cup of carrots diced, one teaspoon of salt, pepper to taste; add two quarts of water and simmer two or three hours. When water has evaporated add soup; if you are making fresh soup, keep adding the "top soup," strained, to the barley and let boil until tender, one-half cup of celery root boiled with the barley improves the flavor.

DRIED PEA SOUP

Soak one cup of picked and cleaned dried split peas in cold water over night, drain, put on with two quarts cold water, a smoked beef-cheek or any other smoked meat; let boil slowly but steadily four hours or more; add one-

Put a small piece of butter in saucepan and then six or eight leeks cut in small pieces. Keep turning for about five minutes so they will get brown; add water for amount desired; season with salt and pepper and put in piece of stale bread. Strain through the strainer. Put in croutons and serve with grated cheese.

RED WINE SOUP

Put on to boil one cup of good red wine and one-half cup of water, sweeten to taste, add three whole cloves and three small pieces of cinnamon bark, let boil ten minutes, and pour while boiling over the well-beaten yolk of one egg. Eat hot or cold. This quantity serves one person.

SPLIT PEA SOUP (MILCHIG)

Soak peas in lukewarm water over night. Use one quart of peas to one gallon of water. Boil about two hours with the following vegetables: a few potatoes, a large celery root, a little parsley and a little onion, a small carrot cut up in cubes and a small clove of garlic. When boiled down to half the quantity, press all through colander. If soup is too thin, take a tablespoon of flour blended with a little cold water in a saucepan and add to the peas already strained. Serve with croutons.

TOMATO SOUP WITH RICE

Brown slightly one minced onion in one tablespoon of butter, add one can of tomatoes or a quart of medium sized tomatoes cut in small pieces, season with salt, pepper, one tablespoon of sugar and a pinch of paprika. Simmer a half hour, strain and thicken with one tablespoon of flour moistened with cold water, add the strained tomatoes and one cup of boiled rice; let come to a boil and serve.

MILK AND CHEESE SOUP

Thicken three cups of milk with one-half tablespoon of flour and cook thoroughly in a double boiler, stirring very often. When ready to serve add one cup of grated cheese and season with salt and paprika.

BLACK BEAN SOUP

Soak one pint of beans over night, drain, add cold water and rinse thoroughly. Fry two tablespoons of chopped onion in two tablespoons of butter, put in with the beans, add two stalks of celery or a piece of celery root and two quarts of water. Cook slowly until the beans are soft, three or four hours, add more boiling water as it boils away; rub through a strainer, add one-eighth teaspoon of pepper, one-fourth teaspoon of mustard, a few grains of cayenne. Heat one tablespoon of butter in saucepan with two tablespoons of flour, then two-thirds cup and then the rest of the soup gradually; cut a lemon (removing seeds) and two hard-boiled eggs in slices and serve in the soup.

BARLEY AND VEGETABLE SOUP

Take a half cup of coarse barley and two quarts of water. Let boil for one hour and skim. Then add two onions, a bunch of carrots, parsley, two turnips, one green pepper and six tomatoes (all chopped fine). Add a few green peas, lima beans, two ears of corn cut from cob; pepper and salt to taste. Cook for one hour or more until done. Then add a small piece of butter, quarter teaspoon of sage and thyme, if you like, and if soup is too thick add more water.

BEER SOUP (PARVE)

Mix the beer with one-third water, boil with sugar and the grated crust of stale rye bread, add stick cinnamon and a little lemon juice. Pour over small pieces of zwieback (rusk). Some boil a handful of dried currants. When done add both currants and juice.

BEET SOUP (RUSSIAN STYLE)

Cut two small beets in strips, cover with water and let cook until tender, add citric acid (sour salt) and a little sugar to make sweet and sour, a little salt, and three-quarter cup of sour cream. Serve cold. Sweet cream may be used and while hot gradually poured over the well-beaten yolks of two eggs, keeping the soup over the stove and stirring all the time until thick and smooth. Remove from stove and serve cold.

CHERRY SOUP

This soup is a summer soup and is to be eaten cold. Cook two tablespoons of sago in one cup of boiling water until tender, add more as water boils down. Put one quart of large red or black cherries, one cup of claret, one tablespoon of broken cinnamon, one-fourth cup of sugar, and one-half lemon sliced fine, up to boil and let boil fifteen minutes; add the cooked sago, let boil up and pour very gradually over the well-beaten yolks of two eggs. Serve cold. Raspberry, strawberry, currant, gooseberry, apple, plum or rhubarb soups are prepared the same way, each cooked until tender and sweetened to taste. The juice of lemon may be used instead of the wine.

FRUIT SOUP

Take two pounds of plums, cherries, or red currants and raspberries, which carefully pick and wash, and boil to a pulp with a pint of water. Let it slightly cool and then stir in the beaten yolk of an egg and a little sugar. Strain the soup, which should be served cold.

COLD SOUR SOUP

Take a pound of sour grass (sorrel), remove leaves, wash well, cut and squeeze well. Peel three potatoes, mince a bunch of young onions, salt and set on to boil, when boiling add the sour grass and let boil well, add two tablespoons of sugar, and a bit of sour salt, let simmer a bit, afterward add two well-beaten eggs. Do not boil this soup after adding the eggs. This soup is to be eaten cold. It can be kept for some time in jars.

GARNISHES AND DUMPLINGS FOR SOUPS

NOODLES

Beat one large egg slightly with one-fourth teaspoon of salt, add enough flour to make a stiff dough; work it well for fifteen or twenty minutes, adding flour when necessary. When the dough is smooth place on slightly floured board and roll out very thin and set aside on a clean towel for an hour or more to dry. Fold in a tight roll and cut crosswise in fine threads. Toss them up lightly with fingers to separate well, and spread them on the board to dry. When thoroughly dry, put in a jar covered with cheese cloth for future use. Drop by handfuls in boiling soup, ten minutes before serving.

Noodles for vegetables or for puddings are made in the same way, but to each egg, one-half egg-shell full of cold water may be added. The strips are cut one-half inch wide.

PLAETCHEN

Take noodle dough, roll out thin in same manner as noodles, when dry cut in three-inch strips, place the strips on top of one another, then cut into one-half inch strips, crosswise, cut again to form one-half inch squares. Dry same as noodles. Drop by handfuls in boiling soup.

KREPLECH OR BUTTERFLIES

Roll noodle dough into pieces two and one-half inches square. Place on each one tablespoon of force-meat, then fold squares into three corned pockets, pressing edges well together. Drop in boiling soup or salted water and boil fifteen minutes.

FORCE-MEAT FOR KREPLECH

Chop one pound of beef, soup meat, cold veal, or take lamb chopped very fine, season with one teaspoon of salt, one-eighth teaspoon of pepper, ginger or nutmeg, one-half teaspoon of onion juice, mix with one egg. This force-meat may also be made into balls one-half inch in diameter, roll the balls in flour and cook them in the boiling soup, or fry them in fat.

BAKING POWDER DUMPLINGS

Sift one cup of flour, one-fourth teaspoon of salt, one teaspoon of baking powder, stir in scant one-half cup of milk or water and mix to a smooth batter. Drop one teaspoonful at a time in the boiling soup; cover kettle, let boil five minutes and serve at once.

CROUTONS

Cut stale bread into cubes, place in pan and brown in the oven; or butter the bread, cut into cubes and then brown the same way. Fry small cubes of stale bread in deep hot fat until brown or fry them in a little butter or fat in a hot spider until brown.

PFÄRVEL OR GRATED EGG FOR SOUP

Into the yolk of one egg stir enough flour until it is too stiff to work. Grate on coarse grater, and spread on board to dry. After soup is strained, put in and boil ten minutes before serving.

SPATZEN

Beat one egg well, add one-half teaspoon of salt, three-fourths cup of flour and one-third cup of water, stirring to a stiff, smooth batter. Drop by teaspoons into boiling soup ten minutes before serving.

EGG CUSTARD

Beat slightly the yolks of two eggs, add two tablespoons of milk and a few grains of salt. Pour into small buttered cup, place in pan of hot water and bake until firm; cool, remove from cup and cut in fancy shapes with French vegetable cutters.

GRATED IRISH POTATO

Peel, wash and grate one large Irish potato, or two medium-sized ones. Put it in a sieve and let hot water run over it until it is perfectly white. Have the white of one egg beaten to a very stiff froth, then stir in the potatoes and twenty minutes before serving add it to the boiling soup. Beat the yolk of one egg up in the soup tureen, and pour the hot soup over it, stirring carefully at first.

FARINA DUMPLINGS

Put in a double boiler one kitchen spoon of fresh butter, stir in one cup of milk. When it begins to boil stir in enough farina to thicken. Take off the stove and when cold add the yolks of two eggs and the stiffly-beaten whites, and a little salt and nutmeg and one-half cup of grated almonds if desired. Let cool, then make into little balls, and ten minutes before soup is to be served, drop in boiler and let boil up once or twice.

BOILED FLOUR BALLS WITH ALMONDS

Two yolks of eggs beaten very light, add a pinch of salt, pepper and finely-chopped parsley. Add six blanched almonds grated, enough sifted flour to make stiff batter, then add the stiffly-beaten whites of eggs and one-half teaspoon of baking powder. Drop by teaspoons in soup ten minutes before serving.

EINLAUF (EGG DROP)

Beat one egg, add one-eighth teaspoon of salt, three tablespoons of flour and one-fourth cup of water, stir until smooth. Pour slowly from a considerable height from the end of a spoon into the boiling soup. Cook two or three minutes and serve hot; add one teaspoon of chopped parsley to the soup.

EGG DUMPLINGS FOR SOUPS

Rub the yolks of two hard-boiled eggs to a smooth paste, add a little salt and grated nutmeg and one-half teaspoon of melted butter. Add the chopped whites of two eggs and a raw egg yolk to be able to mold the dough into little marbles, put in boiling soup one minute.

SCHWEM KLOESSE

Take three tablespoons of flour; stir with one egg and one-half cup of milk; pour this in a pan in which some butter was melted; stir until it loosens from the pan. When it is cold, add two more eggs and some salt, and shortly before needed form in little dumplings and put in boiling hot soup for five minutes.

DUMPLINGS FOR CREAM SOUPS

Scald some flour with milk or water, mix in a small piece of butter and salt, and boil until thick. When cool beat in yolk of an egg, if too stiff add the beaten white.

DROP DUMPLINGS

Break into a cup the whites of three eggs; fill the cup with milk; put it with a tablespoon of fresh butter and one cup of sifted flour in a spider and stir as it boils until it leaves the spider clean. Set aside until cool and stir in the yolks of three eggs. Season with salt, pepper and nutmeg, mix thoroughly and drop by teaspoons in the boiling soup ten minutes before ready to be served.

LIVER KLOESSE (DUMPLINGS)

Brown a small onion minced in one tablespoon of chicken fat, add a small liver chopped fine, chopped parsley, two tablespoons of flour. Season with nutmeg, red and white pepper, and add two eggs. Drop with teaspoon in the boiling soup, let cook ten minutes—serve.

FRITTER BEANS

Beat one egg until light, add three-fourths teaspoon of salt, one-half cup of flour and two tablespoons of water. Put through colander into deep hot fat and fry until brown. Drain and pour hot broth over them.

SPONGE DUMPLINGS

Separate three eggs, beat the yolks, and add one cup of soup stock, one-fourth teaspoon of salt, then add the beaten whites. Pour into a greased cup and place in pan of hot water and steam until firm; cool, remove from cup and cut into small dumplings with a teaspoon; pour the boiling soup over and just before serving add chopped parsley.

FISH

Fish that is not fresh is a very dangerous food and great care should be taken in selecting only fish fit to eat. If the fish is hard in body and the eyes are clear and bright, the gills a bright red and slimy, the flesh so firm that when pressed the marks of the fingers do not remain, the scales not dry or easy to loosen, then the fish is fresh.

In the refrigerator fish will taint butter and other foods if placed in the same compartment, so that in most cases it is better to lay it on a plate on a pan of ice, or wrap it in parchment or waxed paper and put it in the ice box.

Pickerel weighing more than five pounds should not be bought. If belly is thick it is likely that there is another fish inside. This smaller fish or any found in any other fish may not be used as food.

Salt fish should be soaked in fresh water, skin side up, to draw out the salt.

Each fish is at its best in its season, for instance:—

Bluefish, Butterfish, Sea, Striped Bass, Porgies, Sea-trout or Weakfish are best from April to September.

Fluke and Flounders are good all year round, but the fluke is better than the flounder in summer. Carp may be had all year, but care must be taken that it has not been in polluted water.

Cod, Haddock, Halibut, Mackerel, Redsnapper, Salmon, Whitefish are good all year.

In the different states of the United States there are laws governing the fishing for trout, so the season for that fish differs in the various states.

Black Bass, Perch, Pickerel and Pike are in season from June 1st to December 1st.

Shad, April to June.

Smelts, November 10th to April.

TO CLEAN FISH

The fish may be cleaned at the market, but needs to be looked over carefully before cooking.

To remove the scales hold the fish by the tail and scrape firmly toward the head with a small sharp knife, held with the blade slanting toward the tail. Scrape slowly so that the scales will not fly, and rinse the knife frequently in cold water. If the fish is to be served whole, leave the head and tail on and trim the fins; otherwise remove them.

TO OPEN FISH

To open small fish cut under the gills and squeeze out the contents by pressing upward from the middle with the thumb and finger. To open large fish split them from the gills halfway down the body toward the tail; remove the entrails and scrape and clean, opening far enough to remove all the blood from the backbone, and wiping the inside thoroughly with a cloth wrung out of cold, salted water.

TO SKIN FISH

To skin a fish remove the fins along the back and cut off a narrow strip of the skin the entire length of the back. Then slip the knife under the skin that lies over the bony part of the gills and work slowly toward the tail. Do the same with the other side.

TO BONE FISH

To bone a fish clean it first and remove the head. Then, beginning at the tail, run a sharp knife under the flesh close to the bone, scraping the flesh away clean from the bone. Work up one side toward the head; then repeat the same process on the other side of the bone. Lift the bone carefully and pull out any small bones that may be left in the flesh.

BOILED FISH

To cook fish properly is very important, as no food, perhaps, is so insipid as fish if carelessly cooked. It must be well done and properly salted. A good rule to cook fish by is the following: Allow ten minutes to the first pound and five minutes for each additional pound; for example: boil a fish weighing five pounds thirty minutes. By pulling out a fin you may ascertain whether your fish is done; if it comes out easily and the meat is an opaque white, your fish has boiled long enough. Always set your fish on to boil in hot water, hot from the teakettle, adding salt and a dash of vinegar to keep the meat firm; an onion, a head of celery and parsley roots are always an acceptable flavor to any kind of boiled fish, no matter what kind of sauce you intend to serve with the fish. If you wish to serve the fish whole, tie it in a napkin and lay it on an old plate at the bottom of the kettle; if you have a regular "fish kettle" this is not necessary. In boiling fish avoid using too much water.

To thicken sauces, where flour is used, take a level teaspoon of flour to a cup of sauce, or the yolk of an egg to a cup of sauce.

BAKED FISH

Wash and dry the fish, rubbing inside and outside with salt; stuff with a bread stuffing and sew. Sprinkle with salt and pepper and place in a hot oven without water. As soon as it begins to brown add hot water and butter and baste every ten minutes. Bake until done, allowing an hour or more for a large fish, twenty or thirty minutes for a small one. Remove to a hot platter; draw out the strings; garnish with slices of lemon well covered with chopped parsley and serve with Hollandaise sauce.

BROILED FISH

For broiling, large fish should be split down the back and head and tail removed; salmon and halibut should be cut into one-inch slices, and smelts and other small fish left whole. Wipe the fish as dry as possible; sprinkle with salt and pepper and if the fish is dry and white brush the flesh side well with olive oil or butter. Put in a well-greased broiler, placing the thickest parts of the fish toward the middle or back of the broiler. Hold over a hot fire until the flesh side is nicely browned; then cook the skin side just long enough to make the skin crisp. Small fish require from ten to fifteen minutes, large fish from fifteen to twenty-five. To remove from the broiler loosen one side first, then the other, and lift carefully with a cake turner.

Place on a platter; spread with butter and stand in the oven for a few minutes. Garnish with lemon and serve with Maître d'Hôtel butter.

JEWISH METHOD OF FRYING FISH

Scale the fish with the utmost thoroughness, remove the entrails, wash very thoroughly, and salt both inside and out. Then cut the fish into convenient slices, place them on a strainer and leave them there for an hour.

Meanwhile, place some flour in one plate and some beaten eggs in another, and heat a large frying-pan half full of oil or butter. Now wipe your fish slices thoroughly with a clean cloth, dip them first in flour and then in beaten eggs and finally fry until browned.

In frying fish very hot oil is required. If a crumb of bread will brown in twenty seconds the oil is hot enough. Put fish in a frying basket, then into the hot oil and cook five minutes. Drain on brown paper and arrange on platter. Do not stick knife or fork into fish while it is frying.

When the oil has cooled, strain it, pour it into a jar, cover it and it will be ready for use another time. It can be used again for fish only.

ANOTHER METHOD OF FRYING FISH

Thoroughly mix six ounces of flour with an ounce of olive oil, the yolk of an egg, and a pinch of salt. Stir in one gill of tepid water and allow the whole to stand for half an hour in a cool place. Next beat the white of an egg stiff and stir into the batter. Dip each fish into the mixture, then roll in bread crumbs and cook in boiling oil. Butter must not be used. In frying fish do not allow the fish to remain in the spider after it has been nicely browned, for this absorbs the fat and destroys the delicate flavor. Be sure that the fish is done. This rule applies to fish that is sautéd.

SAUTÉD FISH

Clean fish, sprinkle with salt and pepper, dip in flour or cornmeal and cook in spider with just enough hot butter to prevent it sticking to the pan. Shake the pan occasionally. Brown well on under side, then turn and brown on the other side.

LEMON FISH

Boil three tablespoons of vinegar, one sliced onion, six whole peppers, salt, one piece of stick cinnamon, and a little water, then add sliced fish. When fish has boiled twenty minutes remove and arrange on platter. Strain the gravy and add the well-beaten yolks of two eggs, juice of two lemons, sugar to taste and twelve grated almonds. Let all come to a boil, then pour over the fish, sprinkle finely chopped parsley on top and garnish with sliced lemons. Bluefish, mackerel, shad, salmon and porgies may be cooked with this sauce.

SWEET SOUR FISH

First cut up and salt the fish. Shad, trout or carp can be used. Put on fish kettle with one and one-half cups of water and one cup of vinegar, add one onion cut in round slices, one dozen raisins, one lemon cut in round slices, two bay leaves, six cloves. When this mixture begins to boil, lay in your fish and cook thoroughly. When done remove fish to platter.

Put liquor back on stove, add three tablespoons of granulated sugar (which has been melted and browned in a pie plate without water), then add two tablespoons of flour which has been rubbed smooth with a little water. Let boil well and pour over fish. If not sweet enough add more sugar. Serve cold.

SWEET AND SOUR FISH

Place the fish in strong salt water for one hour before cooking. Take three parts of water and one of vinegar, put in saucepan with some sliced onions and some raisins, and let boil until tender. Add brown sugar to taste, a piece of rye bread from which the crust has been removed, and some molasses. Boil the sauce, then place the fish in and let all cook twenty minutes. When done, arrange on platter with sliced lemon and chopped parsley.

SWEET SOUR FISH WITH WINE

Put on to boil in fish kettle, one glass water, one-half glass vinegar, two tablespoons of brown sugar, one-half dozen cloves, one-half teaspoon of ground cinnamon, one onion cut in round slices. Boil thoroughly, then strain and add to it one lemon cut in round slices, one goblet of red wine, one dozen raisins, one tablespoon of pounded almonds; put on stove again, and when it comes to a boil, add fish that has been cut up and salted. Cook until done, remove fish to a platter, and to the liquor add a small piece Lebkuchen or ginger cake, and stir in the well-beaten yolks of four eggs; stir carefully or it will curdle. If not sweet enough add more sugar. Pour over fish. Shad or trout is the best fish to use.

FISH STOCK

Put in a saucepan a tablespoon of butter or butter substitute, add a tablespoon each of chopped onion, carrot and turnip. Fry them without browning, then add fish-bones, head, and trimmings, a stalk of celery, sprigs of parsley and of thyme, a bay-leaf, a tomato or a slice of lemon. Cover with water and let them simmer for an hour or more. Season with salt and pepper and strain.

PIKE WITH EGG SAUCE

Clean the fish thoroughly, and wash it in hot water, wipe dry and salt inside and out. If you heat the salt it will penetrate through the meat of the fish in less time. Take a kettle, lay in it a piece of butter about the size of an egg; cut up an onion, some celery root, parsley root and a few slices of lemon, lay the fish in, either whole or cut up in slices; boil in enough water to just cover the fish, and add more salt if required, add a dozen whole peppers, black or white; season with ground white pepper. Let the fish boil quickly. In the meantime beat up the yolks of two eggs, and pound a dozen almonds to a paste, add to the beaten yolks, together with a tablespoon of cold water. When done remove the fish to a large platter; but to ascertain whether the fish has cooked long enough, take hold of the fins, if they come out readily your fish has cooked enough. Strain the sauce through a sieve, taking out the slices of lemon and with them garnish the top of the fish; add the strained sauce to the beaten eggs, stirring constantly as you do so; then return the sauce to the kettle, and stir until it boils, remove quickly and pour it over the fish. When it is cold garnish with curly parsley.

GEFILLTE FISCH

Prepare trout, pickerel or pike in the following manner: After the fish has been scaled and thoroughly cleaned, remove all the meat that adheres to the skin, being careful not to injure the skin; take out all the meat from head to tail, cut open along the backbone, removing it also; but do not disfigure the head and tail; chop the meat in a chopping bowl, then heat about a quarter of a pound of butter in a spider, add two tablespoons chopped parsley, and some soaked white bread; remove from the fire and add an onion grated, salt, pepper, pounded almonds, the yolks of two eggs, also a very little nutmeg grated. Mix all thoroughly and fill the skin until it looks natural. Boil in salt water, containing a piece of butter, celery root, parsley and an onion; when done remove from the fire and lay on a platter. The fish should be cooked for one and one-quarter hours, or until done. Thicken the sauce with yolks of two eggs, adding a few slices of lemon.

This fish may be baked but must be rolled in flour and dotted with bits of butter.

RUSSIAN FISH CAKES

Take three pounds of fish (weakfish or carp, pickerel or haddock or whitefish, any fat fish with a fish poor in it). Remove skin and bones from the fish and chop flesh very fine, add a good-sized onion, minced or grated, make a depression in the centre of the chopped fish and add three-quarters cup of water, one-half cup of soft bread crumbs, salt and pepper to taste, one-fourth cup of sugar, two egg whites and two tablespoons of melted butter. Chop until very smooth and form into cakes containing a generous tablespoonful each. Put the bones and skins into a saucepan with an onion sliced and a tablespoon of butter and add the fish cakes. Cover with water and simmer for one and a quarter hours. Then remove the cakes and strain off the gravy into the two egg yolks which have been slightly beaten together with one teaspoon of sugar; stir over the heat until thickened, but do not boil it. Pour over fish cakes and serve either hot or cold. The butter and sugar may be omitted if so desired.

GEFILLTE FISCH WITH EGG SAUCE

Cut a five-pound haddock into four-inch slices. Cut a big hole into each slice, preserving the backbone and skin. Put this meat, cut from the fish, into a wooden tray, add to it four large onions and a sprig of parsley. Chop until very fine, then add two eggs, a dash of pepper and cinnamon, a pinch of salt, and a tablespoon of sugar. To this add enough cracker dust to stiffen it. Put this filling into the holes cut in the fish.

Take a saucepan, put in one sliced onion, a sprig of parsley, a small sliced carrot, a dash of pepper, and a pinch of salt. Put the fish into the saucepan, cover with cold water, and let it boil slowly for one hour. At the end of the hour take out the fish, and put on a platter. Preserve the water or gravy in which the fish was boiled for the sauce.

Egg sauce for fish: Beat the yokes of two eggs thoroughly. Into the beaten yolks slowly pour the gravy in which the fish was boiled, stirring constantly. Stand this on the back of the stove to boil for five minutes, stirring constantly so as to prevent burning.

FILLED FISH—TURKISH STYLE

No. 1. Bone some fat fish, boil in salt and water; when done take a little of the fish soup, one egg, beat until light, add gradually the juice of one-half lemon.

FRITADA

No. 2. Steam the fish and bone. Take four good-sized tomatoes, cut them up, add chopped parsley, scallions or leeks cut in small pieces, a little celery, salt and pepper to taste and four eggs well-beaten; mix all these ingredients very well with the boned fish, form in omelet shape. Place in oven in pan greased with olive oil and bake until well browned.

HECHT (PICKEREL)

This fish is best prepared "scharf." Clean your fish thoroughly and salt the day previous; wrap it in a clean towel and lay it on ice until wanted. Line a kettle with celery and parsley roots; cut up an onion, add a lump of fresh butter, and pack the fish in the kettle, head first, either whole or cut up; sprinkle a little salt and white pepper over all and add about a dozen peppercorns; put on enough water to just cover, and add a whole lemon cut in slices. Do not let the fish boil quickly. Add about a dozen pounded almonds. By this time the fish will be ready to turn, then beat up the yolks of two eggs in a bowl, to be added to the sauce after the fish is boiled. Try the fish with a fork and if the meat loosens readily it is done. Take up each peace carefully, if it has been cut up, and arrange on a large platter, head first and so on, make the fish appear whole, and garnish with the slices of lemon and sprigs of parsley; then mince up some parsley and garnish top of the fish, around the lemon slices. Thicken the gravy by adding the beaten yolks, add a tablespoon of cold water to the yolks before adding to the boiling sauce; stir, remove from the fire at once and pour over the fish. If you prefer the sauce strained, then strain before adding the yolks of the eggs and almonds.

Haddock, sea-bass, pike, perch, weakfish and porgies may be cooked "scharf."

FRESH COD OR STRIPED BASS

Cut into pieces ready to serve, after which salt them for an hour. Into the fish kettle put a quantity of water, large onion sliced, carrot also sliced, turnip, celery root, and boil fifteen minutes. Add the fish and two tablespoons of butter, tiny piece of cinnamon, pepper to taste. Boil fifteen minutes longer, then add teaspoon of flour mixed with cold water. Boil up well and add salt or pepper if needed. Remove fish and arrange on platter. Beat yolks of two eggs with a tablespoon of cold water; after straining out vegetables, add the hot gravy in which fish was boiled. Return to fire and stir till thick enough. Garnish with chopped parsley.

AHILADO SAUCE (TURKISH)

Mix some tomato sauce, olive oil, parsley, salt and pepper. Boil sauce first, and add boiled sea-bass or flounders.

BOILED TROUT

Cut up a celery root, one onion, and a sprig of parsley, tie the fish in a napkin and lay it on this bed of roots; pour in enough water to cover and add a dash of vinegar—the vinegar keeps the fish firm—then boil over a quick fire and add more salt to the water in which the fish has been boiled. Lay your fish on a hot platter and prepare the following sauce: set a cup of sweet cream in a kettle, heat it, add a tablespoon of fresh butter, salt and pepper, and thicken with a tablespoon of flour which has been wet with a little cold milk, stir this paste into the cream and boil about one minute, stirring constantly; pour over the fish. Boil two eggs, and while they are boiling, blanch about a dozen or more almonds and stick them into the fish, points up; cover the eggs with cold water, peel them, separate the whites from the yolks, chop each separately; garnish the fish, first with a row of chopped yolks, then whites, until all is used: lay chopped parsley all around the platter.

Fresh cod and striped bass may be cooked in this way.

FISH PIQUANT

Cook any large fish in salt water—salmon is particularly nice prepared in this style—add one cup of vinegar, onions, celery root and parsley. When the fish is cooked enough, remove it from the fire, kettle and all—letting the fish remain in its sauce until the following sauce is prepared:—

Take the yolks of two eggs, one-half teaspoon of Colman's mustard (dry), salt, pepper, a tablespoon of butter, a tablespoon of vinegar, one-half glass water and some fish gravy. Boil in double boiler until thick. Take some parsley, green onions, capers, shallots and one large vinegar pickle and some astragon, chop all up very fine; chop up the hard-boiled whites separately and then add the sauce; mix all this together thoroughly, then taste to see if seasoned to suit.

SALMON CUTLETS

Take the remains of some boiled salmon or a small can of salmon, three tablespoons of mashed potatoes, one of bread crumbs, one of chopped parsley, a little flour, mace, an egg, pepper and salt.

Mix the ingredients well together, bind with the egg, let stand an hour, then form into little flat cutlets, roll in bread crumbs and fry in hot oil, drain on paper and send to table garnished with parsley.

PAPRIKA CARP

Slice and salt three pounds of carp. Steam four sliced onions with one cup of water, to which has been added one teaspoon of paprika, add the sliced carp and cook very slowly until the fish is done.

REDSNAPPER WITH TOMATO SAUCE

Scale thoroughly, salt and pepper inside and out, and lay upon ice, wrapped in a clean cloth overnight. When ready to cook cut up the celery or parsley root, or both, two large onions, a carrot or two, and let this come to a boil in about one quart of water, then lay in the fish, whole or in pieces; let the water almost cover the fish; add a lump of fresh butter and three or four tomatoes (out of season you may use canned tomatoes, say three or four large spoonfuls); let the fish boil half an hour, turning it occasionally. Try it by taking hold of the fins, if they come out readily, the fish is done. Take it up carefully; lay on a large platter and strain the sauce; let it boil, thicken it with the well-beaten yolks of two eggs, adding the sauce gradually to the eggs and stirring constantly. Garnish the fish with chopped parsley, letting a quantity mix with the sauce.

Redsnapper is also very good fried.

BONED SMELTS, SAUTÉD

Take a dozen raw smelts; split them from the back lengthwise, leaving the head and tail intact; take out the large center bone without opening the stomach and season with salt. Put four ounces of butter into a saucepan, and when quite hot place the smelts in it, so that the side which was cut open is underneath. When they have attained a nice color, turn them over and finish cooking. When ready, arrange them on a very hot dish, pour the butter in which they were cooked over them, squeeze a little lemon on them, then add over all some finely chopped green parsley. Serve.

FISH WITH HORSERADISH SAUCE

Clean three pounds of fresh salmon, bone, salt and let stand several hours. Place in fish kettle with boiling salt water (one teaspoon of salt to one quart of water), and let boil one-half hour or until well cooked. Lift out carefully, place on hot platter and pour over one-fourth cup of melted butter and sprinkle well with one tablespoon of parsley. Serve in a separate bowl the following sauce; a large spoonful with each portion of fish: Peel one-half pound of horseradish root, grate and mix well with one pint of cream beaten stiff. The fish must be hot and the sauce cold.

FISH WITH SAUERKRAUT

Fry an onion in butter (or vegetable oil), add sauerkraut and cook. Boil the fish in salt water, then bone and shred. Fry two minced onions in butter or oil, put them into the kettle with the fish, add two egg yolks, butter or oil, a little pepper and a tablespoon of breadcrumbs; steam for half hour and serve with the kraut.

FILLET OF SOLE À LA MOUQUIN

Thoroughly wash and pick over a pound of spinach, put it over the fire with no more water than clings to the leaves and cook for ten minutes; at the end of that time drain the spinach and chop it fine. Have ready thin fillets of flounder, halibut, or whitefish. Cover them with acidulated warm water—a slice of lemon in the water is all that is wanted, and add a slice of onion, a sprig of parsley and a bit of bay leaf. Simmer for ten minutes and drain. Put the minced spinach into the bottom of the buttered baking-dish, arrange the fillets on it, cover with a cream sauce to which a tablespoon of grated cheese has been added, and brown in the oven.

FILLET DE SOLE À LA CREOLE

Fillet some large flounders, and have fishman send you all the bones; put the bones on to boil; wash, dry, and season the fillets; roll them (putting in some bits of butter), and fasten each one with a wooden toothpick. Strain the water from the bones; thicken with a little brown flour and onion; add to this one-half can of tomatoes, a little cayenne pepper, salt, and chopped green peppers. Let this sauce simmer for a couple of hours (this need not be strained); put the fillets in a casserole, and pour some of this sauce over them, and put in the oven for about fifteen minutes. Then pour over the rest of the tomato sauce, sprinkle a little chopped parsley and serve. One can add a few mushrooms to the sauce. The mushrooms must be fried in butter before being added to the sauce.

BAKED BLACK BASS

After having carefully cleaned, salt well and lay it in the baking-pan with a small cup of water, and strew flakes of butter on top, also salt, pepper and a little chopped parsley. Bake about one hour, basting often until brown. Serve on a heated platter; garnish with parsley and lemon and make a sauce by adding a glass of sherry, a little catsup and thicken with a teaspoon of flour, adding this to fish gravy. Serve potatoes with fish, boiled in the usual way, making a sauce of two tablespoons of butter. Add a bunch of parsley chopped very fine, salt and pepper to taste, a small cup of sweet cream thickened with a tablespoon of flour. Pour over potatoes.

BAKED FLOUNDERS

Clean, wipe dry, add salt and pepper and lay them in a pan; put flakes of butter on top, an onion cut up, some minced celery and a few bread crumbs. A cup of hot water put into the pan will prevent burning. Baste often; bake until brown.

BAKED BASS À LA WELLINGTON

Remove the scales and clean. Do not remove the head, tail, or fins. Put into a double boiler one tablespoon of butter, two cups of stale bread crumbs, one tablespoon of chopped onion, one teaspoon of chopped parsley, two teaspoons of chopped capers, one-fourth cup of sherry. Heat all the above ingredients, season with paprika and salt, and stuff the bass with the mixture. Sew up the fish, put into a hot oven, bake and baste with sherry wine and butter.

A fish weighing four or five pounds is required for the above recipe.

BAKED FISH—TURKISH STYLE

Take perch and stuff with steamed onion to which has been added one well-beaten egg, two tomatoes cut up in small pieces, some bread crumbs, chopped parsley or celery, salt and pepper to taste. Bake until the fish is nicely browned.

SAUCE AGRISTOGA

Fry any fish in oil, and serve the following:—

Beat very well two whole eggs, add two tablespoons of flour diluted with cold water, add gradually the juice of one lemon.

ZUEMIMO SAUCE

Heat one teaspoon of oil, add one tablespoon of flour, add slowly one-half cup of vinegar diluted with water; season with salt and sugar. If no other fish can be procured, salt herring may be used.

SHAD ROE

Parboil the roe in salted water ten minutes. Drain; season with salt, pepper and melted butter; form into balls, roll in beaten egg and cracker crumbs and fry in hot oil or any butter substitute.

The roe can be baked and served with tomato sauce.

BAKED SHAD

Clean and split a three-pound shad. Place in a buttered dripping pan. Sprinkle with salt and pepper, brush with melted butter and bake in a hot oven thirty minutes.

SCALLOPED FISH ROE

Boil three large roes in water with a little vinegar for ten minutes. Plunge into cold water; wipe the roe dry. Mash the yolks of three hard-boiled eggs into a cup of melted butter, teaspoon of anchovy paste, tablespoon of chopped parsley, juice of half a lemon, salt and pepper to taste. Add a cup of bread crumbs and then mix in lightly the roe that has been broken into pieces. Put all in baking dish, cover with bread crumbs and flakes of butter, and brown in oven.

BAKED MACKEREL

Split fish, clean, and remove head and tail. Put in buttered pan, sprinkle with salt and pepper and dot over with butter (allowing one tablespoon to a medium-sized fish), pour over two-thirds of a cup of milk. Bake twenty-five minutes in a hot oven.

STUFFED HERRING

Make a dressing of two tablespoons of bread crumbs, one tablespoon of chopped parsley, two tablespoons of butter, juice of one-half lemon, and pepper and salt to taste. Add enough hot water to make soft. Fill the herrings, roll up, tie in shape. Cover with greased paper and bake ten to fifteen minutes.

FISH WITH GARLIC

Clean, salt fish one half hour, wash and dry with a clean cloth; cut garlic very thin, rub over fish; place in oven to bake; bake until odor of garlic has disappeared; then let fish cool.

BAKED CHOPPED HERRING

Soak herring one hour in water and then one and a half in sweet milk, skin, bone and chop; cut up a medium-sized onion, fry in butter until golden brown, add a cup of cream, two egg yolks and one-fourth cup of white bread crumbs, then put in a little more cream. Butter pan, sprinkle with crumbs or cracker dust, then put in herring, pepper slightly. Bake in moderate oven three-quarters of an hour.

MARINIRTE (PICKLED) HERRING

Take new Holland herring, remove the heads and scales, wash well, open them and take out the milch and lay the herring and milch in milk or water over night. Next day lay the herring in a stone jar with alternate layers of onions cut up, also lemon cut in slices, a few cloves, whole peppers and a few bay leaves, some capers and whole mustard seed. Take the milch and rub it through a hair sieve, the more of them you have the better for the sauce; stir in a spoon of brown sugar and vinegar and pour it over the herring.

SALT HERRING

Soak salt herring over night in cold water, that the salt may be drawn out. Drain and serve with boiled potatoes, or bone and place in kettle of cold water, let come to a boil and let simmer a few minutes until tender, drain and pour melted butter over them and serve hot with boiled or fried potatoes.

BROILED SALT MACKEREL

Freshen the fish by soaking it over night in cold water, with the skin uppermost. Drain and wipe dry, remove the head and tail; place it upon a butter broiler, and slowly broil to a light brown. Place upon a hot dish, add pepper, bits of butter, a sprinkling of parsley and a little lemon juice.

BOILED SALT MACKEREL

Soak mackerel over night in cold water, with the skin side up, that the salt may be drawn out, change the water often, and less time is required. Drain. Place mackerel in shallow kettle, pour water over to cover and boil ten to fifteen minutes or until flesh separates from the bone. Remove to platter and pour hot, melted butter over and serve with hot potatoes.

They may also be boiled and served with a White Sauce.

MARINIRTE FISH

Take pickerel, pike or any fish that is not fat, cut into two-inch slices, wash well, salt and set aside in a cool place for a few hours. When ready to cook, wash slightly so as not to remove all salt from fish. Take heads and set up to boil with a whole onion for twenty-five minutes, then add the other pieces and two cups of vinegar, one cup of water, four bay leaves and twelve allspice, a little pepper and ginger. Cook for thirty-five minutes longer. Taste fish, add a little water or a little more vinegar to taste. Then remove fish carefully so as not to break the pieces and let cool. Strain the sauce, return fish to same, adding a few bay leaves and allspice. Set in a cool place until sauce forms a jelly around the fish. Can be kept covered and in a cool place for some time.

SOUSED HERRING

Split and half three herrings, roll and tie them up. Place them in a pie plate, pour over them a cup of vinegar, add whole peppers, salt, cloves to taste and two bay leaves. Bake in a slow oven until soft (about twenty minutes).

SALMON LOAF

Blend together one can of salmon, one cup of grated bread crumbs, two beaten eggs, one cup of milk, one teaspoon of lemon juice, one-half teaspoon of paprika, one-half teaspoon of salt, one tablespoon of chopped parsley and one tablespoon of onion juice. Place in a greased baking dish. Sprinkle top with thin layer of bread crumbs. Bake in hot oven for thirty minutes or until the crumbs that cover the dish are browned. Serve with a white sauce.

CREAM SALMON

Remove salmon from the can, place it in a colander and wash under running water or scald with boiling water. Break into small pieces, stir into one cup of hot cream sauce; bring all to a boil and serve in patty cups or on toasted bread or crackers.

PICKLE FOR SALMON

Take equal parts of vinegar, white wine and water. Boil these with a little mace, a clove or two, a bit of ginger root, one or two whole peppers and some grated horseradish. Take out the last named ingredient when sufficiently boiled, and pour the pickle over the salmon, previously boiled in strong salt and water.

KEDGEREE

Cut up in small pieces about a pound of any kind of cooked fish except herring. Boil two eggs hard and chop up. Take one cup of rice and boil in the following manner:—After washing it well and putting it on in boiling water, with a little salt, let it boil for ten minutes, drain it almost dry and let it steam with the lid closely shut for ten minutes longer without stirring.

Take a clean pot and put in the fish, eggs, rice, a good dessertspoon of butter, and pepper and salt to taste. Stir over the fire until quite hot. Press into a mould and turn it out at once and serve.

SWISS CREAMED FISH

Mix smoothly in one cup of cold water a teaspoon of flour. Stir it into one cup of boiling milk and when thick and smooth add the meat of any cold fish, picked free from skin and bones. Season with salt, pepper and a tablespoon of butter. If the cream is desired to be extra rich one well-beaten egg may be added one minute before removing from the fire. Serve hot. A pinch of cayenne or a saltspoon of paprika is relished by many.

COD FISH BALLS

Put the fish to soak over night in lukewarm water. Change again in the morning and wash off all the salt. Cut into pieces and boil about fifteen minutes, pour off this water and put on to boil again with boiling water. Boil twenty minutes this time, drain off every bit of water, put on a platter to cool and pick to pieces as fine as possible, removing every bit of skin and bone. When this is done, add an equal quantity of mashed potatoes, a tablespoon of butter, a very little salt and pepper, beat up one egg and a little milk, if necessary, mix with a fork. Flour your hands well and form into biscuit-shaped balls. Fry in hot oil.

FINNAN HADDIE

Parboil ten minutes and then broil like fresh fish.

To bake, place the fish in a pan, add one cup of milk and one cup of water; cover. Cook ten minutes in hot oven. Remove cover, drain, spread with butter and season with pepper.

FINNAN HADDIE AND MACARONI

Break up and cook until tender about a package of macaroni. Pick up the finnan haddie until you have about three-quarters as much as you have macaroni. Mix in a greased baking-dish and pour over a drawn butter sauce, made with cornstarch or with any good milk or cream dressing, then cover with bread or cracker crumbs or leave plain to brown in oven. Bake from twenty to thirty minutes.

SCALLOPED FISH, No. 1

Line a buttered baking-dish with cold flaked fish. Sprinkle with salt and pepper; add a layer of cold cooked rice, dot with butter; repeat and cover with cracker or bread crumbs. Bake fifteen to twenty minutes.

SCALLOPED FISH, No. 2

Butter a dish, place in a layer of cold cooked fish, sprinkle with bread crumbs, parsley, salt, butter and pepper; repeat. Cover with white sauce, using one tablespoon of flour to two tablespoons of butter and one cup of milk. Sprinkle top with buttered bread crumbs and bake.

SAUCES FOR FISH AND VEGETABLES

These sauces are made by combining butter and flour and thinning with water or other liquid. A sauce should never be thickened by adding a mixture of flour and water, as in that case the flour is seldom well cooked; or by adding flour alone, as this way is certain to cause lumps. The flour should be allowed to cook before the liquid is added.

All sauces containing butter and milk should be cooked in a double boiler.

If so desired, any neutral oil—that is, vegetable or nut oil—may be substituted for the butter called for in the recipe.

Care in preparation of a sauce is of as much importance as is the preparation of the dish the sauce garnishes.

DRAWN BUTTER SAUCE

Melt two tablespoons of butter and stir in two tablespoons of flour. Add carefully one cup of boiling water, then season with one-half teaspoon of salt and a dash of pepper and paprika.

Many sauces are made with drawn butter as a foundation. For caper sauce add three tablespoons of capers.

For egg sauce add one egg, hard-boiled and chopped fine.

BEARNAISE SAUCE

There are several ways of making Bearnaise sauce. This is one very simple rule: Bring to the boil two tablespoons each of vinegar and water. Simmer in it for ten minutes a slice of onion. Take out the onion and add the yolks of three eggs beaten very light. Take from the fire, add salt and pepper to season, and four tablespoons of butter beaten to a cream, and added slowly.

Quick Bearnaise Sauce.—Beat the yolks of four eggs with four tablespoons of oil and four of water. Add a cup of boiling water and cook slowly until thick and smooth. Take from the fire, and add minced onion, capers, olives, pickles, and parsley and a little tarragon vinegar.

CUCUMBER SAUCE

Pare two large cucumbers; remove seeds, if large; chop fine and squeeze dry. Season with salt, vinegar, paprika and add one-half cup of cream.

SAUCE HOLLANDAISE

Mix one tablespoon of butter and one of flour in a saucepan and add gradually half a pint of boiling water. Stir until it just reaches the boiling point; take from the fire and add the yolks of two eggs. Into another saucepan put a slice of onion, a bay leaf, and a clove of garlic; add four tablespoons of vinegar, and stand this over the fire until the vinegar is reduced one-half. Turn this into the sauce, stir for a moment; strain through a fine sieve; add half a teaspoon of salt and serve. This sauce may be varied by adding lemon juice instead of vinegar, or by using the water in which the fish was boiled. It is one of the daintiest of all sauces.

MUSTARD SAUCE

Mix two tablespoons of vinegar and one of mustard, one teaspoon of oil or butter melted, pepper and salt to taste. Add this to two hard-boiled eggs chopped fine, with a small onion and about the same quantity of parsley as eggs; and mix all well together.

MAÎTRE D'HÔTEL BUTTER

Work into one-half cup of butter all the lemon juice it will take, and add a teaspoon of minced parsley.

PICKLE SAUCE

Cream two tablespoons of butter, add one teaspoon of salt and one tablespoon of chopped pickle. A speck of red pepper may be added.

SARDELLEN, OR HERRING SAUCE

Brown a spoon of flour in heated fat, add a quantity of hot fish stock and a few sardellen chopped fine, which you have previously washed in cold water, also a finely-chopped onion. Let this boil a few minutes, add a little vinegar and sugar; strain this sauce through a wire sieve and add a few capers and a wineglass of white wine and let it boil up once again and thicken with the yolk of one egg.

SAUCE VINAIGRETTE

Rub the mixing bowl with a clove of garlic, add one-half teaspoon of salt, dash of white pepper, and a teaspoon of cold water or a bit of ice, then four tablespoons of oil. Mix until the salt is dissolved, remove the ice and add ten drops of tabasco sauce, two tablespoons tarragon vinegar, one tablespoon grated onion, one tablespoon chopped parsley and one chopped gherkin.

ANCHOVY SAUCE

Mix six tablespoons of melted butter and one and one-half teaspoons anchovy paste, place in double boiler and allow to boil for about six minutes. Flavor with lemon juice.

SAUCE PIQUANTE

To one pint of drawn butter add one tablespoon each of vinegar and lemon juice and two tablespoons each of chopped capers, pickles, and olives, one-half teaspoon onion juice, a few grains cayenne pepper.

SAUCE TARTARE

Add to a half pint of well-made mayonnaise dressing two olives, one gherkin and one small onion, chopped fine. Chop sufficient parsley to make a tablespoonful, crush it in a bowl and add it first to the mayonnaise. Stir in at least a tablespoon of drained capers and serve with fried or broiled fish.

FRYING

PREPARED BREAD CRUMBS FOR FRYING

All scraps of bread should be saved for crumbs, the crusts being separated from the white part, then dried, rolled, and sifted, and put away until needed in a covered glass jar.

The brown crumbs are good for the first coating, the white ones for the outside, as they give better color. Cracker crumbs give a smooth surface, but for most things bread crumbs are preferable.

For meats a little salt and pepper, and for sweet articles, a little sugar, should be mixed with the crumbs. Crumbs left on the board should be dried, sifted, and kept to be used again.

FRYING

Frying is cooking in very hot fat or oil, and the secret of success is to have the fat hot enough to harden the outer surface of the article to be fried immediately and deep enough to cover these articles of food. As the fat or oil can be saved and used many times, the use of a large quantity is not extravagant.

To fry easily one must have, in addition to the deep, straight-sided frying-pan, a frying-basket, made from galvanized wire, with a side handle. The bale handles are apt to become heated, and in looking for something to lift them, the foods are over-fried. The frying-pan must be at least six inches deep with a flat bottom; iron, granite ware or copper may be used, the first two are preferable. There must be sufficient fat to wholly cover the articles fried, but the pan must not be too full, or there is danger of overflow when heavy articles are put in. After each frying, drain the fat or oil, put it into a receptacle kept for the purpose, and use it over and over again as long as it lasts. As the quantity begins to lessen, add sufficient fresh fat or oil to keep up the amount.

Always put the fat or oil in the frying-pan before you stand it over the fire.

Wait until it is properly heated before putting in the articles to be fried.

Fry a few articles at a time. Too many will cool the fat or oil below the point of proper frying and they will absorb grease and be unpalatable.

Put articles to be fried in the wire frying-basket and lower into the boiling hot fat or oil. Test the fat by lowering a piece of stale bread into it, if the bread browns in thirty seconds the fat is sufficiently hot.

Fry croquettes a light brown; drain over the fat, lift the frying-basket from the hot fat to a round plate, remove the articles from the basket quickly to brown paper, drain a moment and serve.

When frying fish or any food that is to be used at a milk meal, use oil. Olive oil is the best, but is very expensive for general use. Any other good vegetable oil or nut oil will do as substitute.

When the food is intended for a meat meal; fat may be prepared according to the following directions and used in the same manner as oil.

TO RENDER GOOSE, DUCK OR BEEF FAT

Cut the fat into small pieces. Put in a deep, iron kettle and cover with cold water. Place on the stove uncovered; when the water has nearly all evaporated, set the kettle back and let the fat try out slowly. When the fat is still and scraps are shriveled and crisp at the bottom of the kettle, strain the fat through a cloth into a stone crock, cover and set it away in a cool place. The water may be omitted and the scraps slowly tried out on back of stove or in moderate oven. When fat is tried out, pour in crock.

Several slices of raw potato put with the fat will aid in the clarifying.

All kinds of fats are good for drippings except mutton fat, turkey fat and fat from smoked meats which has too strong a flavor to be used for frying, but save it with other fat that may be unsuitable for frying, and when six pounds are collected make it into hard soap.

TO MAKE WHITE HARD SOAP

Save every scrap of fat each day; try out all that has accumulated; however small the quantity. This is done by placing the scraps in a frying-pan on the back of the range. If the heat is low, and the grease is not allowed to get hot enough to smoke or burn, there will be no odor from it. Turn the melted grease into tin pails and keep them covered. When six pounds of fat have been obtained, turn it into a dish-pan; add a generous amount of hot water, and stand it on the range until the grease is entirely melted. Stir it well together; then stand it aside to cool. This is clarifying the grease. The clean grease will rise to the top, and when it has cooled can be taken off in a cake, and such impurities as have not settled in the water can be scraped off the bottom of the cake of fat.

Put the clean grease into the dish-pan and melt it. Put a can of Babbitt's lye in a tin pail; add to it a quart of cold water, and stir it with a stick or wooden spoon until it is dissolved. It will get hot when the water is added; let it stand until it cools. Remove the melted grease from the fire, and pour in the lye slowly, stirring all the time. Add two tablespoons of ammonia. Stir the mixture constantly for twenty minutes or half an hour, or until the soap begins to set.

Let it stand until perfectly hard; then cut it into square cakes. This makes a very good, white hard soap which will float on water.

ENTRÉES

CROQUETTES

Combine ingredients as directed in the recipe, roll the mixture lightly between the hands into a ball. Have a plentiful supply of bread crumbs spread evenly on a board; roll the ball lightly on the crumbs into the shape of a cylinder, and flatten each end by dropping it lightly on the board; put it in the egg (to each egg add one tablespoon of water, and beat together), and with a spoon moisten the croquette completely with the egg; lift it out on a knife-blade, and again roll lightly in the crumbs. Have every part entirely covered, so there will be no opening through which the grease may be absorbed. Where a light yellow color is wanted, use fresh white crumbs grated from the loaf (or rubbed through a purée sieve) for the outside, and do not use the yolk of the egg. Coarse fresh crumbs are used for fish croquettes, which are usually made in the form of chops, or half heart shape. A small hole is pricked in the pointed end after frying, and a sprig of parsley inserted. Have all the croquettes of perfectly uniform size and shape, and lay them aside on a dish, not touching one another, for an hour or more before frying. This will make the crust more firm.

The white of an egg alone may be used for egging them, but not the yolk alone. Whip the egg with the water, just enough to break it, as air-bubbles in the egg will break in frying, and let the grease penetrate. Serve the croquettes on a platter, spread them on a napkin and garnish with sprigs of parsley.

CHICKEN CROQUETTES, No. 1

Cook one-half tablespoon of flour in one tablespoon chicken-fat, add one-half cup of soup stock gradually, and one-half teaspoon each of onion juice, lemon juice, salt, and one-quarter teaspoon of pepper, one and one-half cups of veal or chicken, chopped very fine, one pair of brains which have been boiled, mix these well, remove from the fire and add one well-beaten egg. Turn this mixture out on a flat dish and place in ice-box to cool. Then roll into small cones, dip in beaten egg, roll again in powdered bread or cracker crumbs and drop them into boiling fat, fry until a delicate brown.

CHICKEN CROQUETTES, No. 2

Chop the chicken very fine, using the white meat alone, or the dark meat alone, or both together. Season with salt, pepper, onion-juice, and lemon-juice. Chopped mushrooms, sweetbreads, calf's brains, tongue, or truffles are used with chicken, and a combination of two or more of them much improves the quality of the croquettes.

CROQUETTES OF CALF'S BRAINS

Lay the brains in salt water an hour, or until they look perfectly white, then take out one at a time, pat with your hands to loosen the outer skin and pull it off. Beat or rub them to a smooth paste with a wooden spoon, season with salt and pepper and a very little mace; add a beaten egg and about one-half cup of bread crumbs. Heat fat in a spider and fry large spoonfuls of this mixture in it.

MEAT CROQUETTES

Veal, mutton, lamb, beef and turkey croquettes may be prepared in the same way as chicken croquettes.

MEAT AND BOILED HOMINY CROQUETTES

Equal proportions.

SWEETBREAD CROQUETTES

Cut the boiled sweetbreads into small dice with a silver knife. Mix with mushrooms, using half the quantity of mushrooms that you have of sweetbreads. Use two eggs in the sauce.

VEAL CROQUETTES

Veal is often mixed with chicken, or is used alone as a substitute for chicken. Season in same manner and make the same combinations.

CAULIFLOWER CROQUETTES

Finely chop cold cooked cauliflower, mix in one small, finely chopped onion, one small bunch of parsley finely chopped, one-half cup of bread crumbs and one well-beaten egg. Carefully mix and mold into croquette forms, dip in cracker dust and fry in deep, smoking fat until a light brown.

EGGPLANT CROQUETTES (ROUMANIAN)

Peel the eggplant, place in hot water and boil until tender, drain, add two eggs, salt, pepper, two tablespoons of matzoth or white flour or bread crumbs, beat together; fry in butter or oil by tablespoonfuls.

CROQUETTES OF FISH

Take any kind of boiled fish, separate it from the bones carefully, chop with a little parsley, salt and pepper to taste. Beat up one egg with one teaspoon of milk and flour. Roll the fish into balls and turn them in the beaten egg and cracker crumbs or bread. Fry a light brown. Serve with any sauce or a mayonnaise.

POTATO CROQUETTES

Work into two cups of mashed potatoes, a tablespoon of melted butter, until smooth and soft; add one egg well-beaten and beat all together with a wooden spoon. Season with salt and nutmeg. Roll each in beaten egg then in bread crumbs, fry in hot oil or butter substitute. If desired chicken-fat may be substituted for the butter and the croquettes fried in deep fat or oil.

SWEET POTATO CROQUETTES

Press through a ricer sufficient hot baked sweet potatoes to measure one pint. Place over the fire. Add one teaspoon of butter or drippings, the beaten yolks of two eggs, pepper and salt to taste, and beat well with a fork until the mixture leaves the sides of the pan. Cool slightly, form into cones, roll in fine bread crumbs; dip in beaten eggs, roll again in crumbs and fry in hot oil or fat.

PEANUT AND RICE CROQUETTES

To one cup of freshly cooked rice allow one cup of peanut butter, four tablespoons of minced celery, one teaspoon of grated onion, one tablespoon of canned tomatoes, and salt and pepper to taste. Mix well; add the white of one egg, reserving the yolk for coating the croquettes. Shape into croquettes and let stand in a cold place for an hour, then coat with the egg yolk mixed with one tablespoon of water and roll in stale bread crumb dust until well covered. Fry in any hot oil or butter substitute.

RICE CROQUETTES, No. 1

Separate the white and yolk of one egg and reserve about half the yolk for coating the croquette. Beat the rest with the white. Mix with two cups of boiled or steamed rice and one-half teaspoon of salt, form into oblong croquettes or small balls. Mix the reserved part of the egg yolk with a tablespoon of cold water. Dip croquettes in this and then roll in fine bread crumbs. Repeat until well-coated, then fry brown in deep oil.

RICE CROQUETTES, No. 2

Put on with cold water one cup of rice, and let boil until tender. Drain, and mix with the rice, one tablespoon of butter, yolks of three eggs, and pinch of salt. About one tablespoon of flour may be added to hold the croquettes together. Beat the whites of the three eggs to a stiff froth, reserving some of the beaten white for egging croquettes, mix this in last, shape into croquettes and fry in hot oil or butter substitute. Place on platter and serve with a lump of jelly on each croquette.

CALF'S BRAINS (SOUR)

Lay the brains in ice-water and then skin. They will skin easily by taking them up in your hands and patting them, this will help to loosen all the skin and clotted blood that adheres to them. Lay in cold salted water for an hour at least, then put on to boil in half vinegar and half water (a crust of rye bread improves the flavor of the sauce). Add one onion, cut up fine, ten whole peppers, one bay leaf, one or two cloves and a little salt, boil altogether about fifteen minutes. Serve on a platter and decorate with parsley. Eat cold.

CALF'S BRAINS FRIED

Clean as described in calf's brains cooked sour; wipe dry, roll in rolled cracker flour, season with salt and pepper and fry as you would cutlets.

BRAINS (SWEET AND SOUR)

Clean as described above. Lay in ice-cold salted water for an hour. Cut up an onion, a few slices of celery root, a few whole peppers, a little salt and a crust of rye bread. Lay the brains upon this bed of herbs and barely cover with vinegar and water. Boil about fifteen minutes, then lift out the brains, with a perforated skimmer, and lay upon a platter to cool. Take a "lebkuchen," some brown sugar, a tablespoon of molasses, one-half teaspoon of cinnamon, a few seedless raisins and a few pounded almonds. Moisten this with vinegar and add the boiling sauce. Boil the sauce ten minutes longer and pour scalding over the brains. Eat cold and decorate with slices of lemon.

DEVILED BRAINS

Put one tablespoon of fat in skillet, and when hot add two tablespoons of flour, rub until smooth, and brown lightly, then add one-half can of tomatoes, season with salt, pepper, finely-chopped parsley, and a dash of cayenne pepper, and the brains which have previously been cleaned, scalded with boiling water, and cut in small pieces. Cook a few minutes, and then fill the shells with the mixture. Over each shell sprinkle bread crumbs, and a little chicken-fat. Put shells in pan and brown nicely. Serve with green peas.

BRAINS WITH EGG SAUCE

Wash brains well, skin, boil fifteen minutes in salt water; slice in stew-pan some onions, salt, pepper, ginger and a cup of stock. Put in the brains with a little marjoram; let it cook gently for one-half hour. Mix yolks of two eggs, juice of a lemon, a teaspoon of flour, a little chopped parsley; when it is rubbed smooth, stir it into saucepan; stir well to prevent curdling.

JELLIED CHICKEN

Boil a chicken in as little water as possible until the meat falls from the bones, chop rather fine and season with pepper and salt. Put into a mold a layer of the chopped meat and then a layer of hard-boiled eggs, cut in slices. Fill the mold with alternate layers of meat and eggs until nearly full. Boil down the liquor left in the kettle until half the quantity. While warm, add one-quarter of a cup aspic, pour into the mold over the meat. Set in a cool place overnight to jelly.

PRESSED CHICKEN

Boil one or more chickens just as you would for fricassee, using as little water as possible. When tender remove all the meat from the bone and take off all the skin. Chop as fine as possible in a chopping bowl (it ought to be chopped as fine as powder). Add all the liquor the chicken was boiled in, which ought to be very little and well seasoned. Press it into the shape of a brick between two platters, and put a heavy weight over it so as to press hard. Set away to cool in ice-chest and garnish nicely with parsley and slices of lemon before sending to the table. It should be placed whole upon the table, and sliced as served. Serve pickles and olives with it. Veal may be pressed in the same way, some use half veal and half chicken, which is equally nice.

HOME-MADE CHICKEN TAMALES

Boil till tender one large chicken. Have two quarts of stock left when chicken is done. Remove chicken and cut into medium-sized pieces. Into the stock pour gradually one cup of corn meal or farina, stirring until it thickens. If not the proper consistency, add a little more meal. Season with one tablespoon of chili sauce, three tablespoons of tomato catsup, salt, one teaspoon of Spanish pepper sauce. Simmer gently thirty minutes, then add chicken. Serve in ramekins.

CHICKEN FRICASSEE, WITH NOODLES

Prepare a rich "Chicken Fricassee" (recipe for which you will find among poultry recipes), but have a little more gravy than usual. Boil some noodles or macaroni in salted water, drain, let cold water run through them, shake them well and boil up once with chicken. Serve together on a large platter.

SWEETBREAD GLACÉ, SAUCE JARDINIÈRE WITH SPAGHETTI

Put on some poultry drippings to heat in a saucepan, cut up an onion, shredded very fine and then put in the sweetbreads, which have been picked over carefully and lain in salt water an hour before boiling. Salt and pepper the sweetbreads before putting in the kettle, slice two tomatoes on top and cover up tight and set on the back of stove to simmer slowly. Turn once in a while and add a little soup stock. Boil one-half cup of string beans, half a can of canned peas, one-half cup of currants, cut up extremely fine, with a tablespoon of drippings, a little salt and ground ginger. When the vegetables are tender, add to the simmering sweetbreads. Thicken the sauce with a teaspoon of flour. Have the sauce boiled down quite thick. Boil the spaghetti in salted water until tender. Serve with the sweetbreads.

CHICKEN À LA SWEETBREAD

Take the breast of chicken that has been fricasseed, cut up into small pieces, and add mushrooms. Make brown sauce. Serve in paté shells.

SWEETBREADS

Wash the sweetbreads very carefully and remove all bits of skin and fatty matter. Cover with cold water, salt and boil for fifteen minutes. Then remove from the boiling water and cover with cold water. Sprinkle with salt and pepper, roll in beaten egg and bread crumbs, and fry a nice brown in hot fat.

SWEETBREAD SAUTÉ WITH MUSHROOMS

Clean sweetbread, boil until tender, and cut in small pieces. Take one tablespoon of fat, blend in one tablespoon of flour; add half the liquor of a can of mushrooms and enough soup stock to make the necessary amount of gravy; add a little catsup, mushroom catsup, and a few drops of kitchen bouquet, a clove of garlic, and a small onion; salt and pepper to taste. Cook this about an hour, and then remove garlic and onion. Add sweetbreads, mushrooms, and two hard-boiled eggs chopped very fine.

VEAL SWEETBREADS (FRIED)

Wash and lay your sweetbreads in slightly salted cold water for an hour; Pull off carefully all the outer skin, wipe dry and sprinkle with salt and pepper. Heat some goose-fat in a spider, lay in the sweetbreads and fry slowly on the back of the stove, turning frequently until they are a nice brown.

CALF'S FEET, PRUNES AND CHESTNUTS

Two calf's feet, sawed into joints, seasoned with pepper and salt a day before using. Place in an iron pot, one-half pound Italian chestnuts that have been scalded and skinned, then the calf's feet, one-eighth pound of raisins, one pound of fine prunes, one small onion, one small head of celery root, two olives cut in small pieces, one-eighth teaspoon of paprika, one cup of soup stock. Stew slowly for five hours, and add one hour before serving, while boiling, a wine glass claret and a wine glass sherry. Do not stir.

CALF'S FEET, SCHARF

Take calf's feet, saw into joints; put on to boil within cold water and boil slowly until the gristle loosens from the bones. Season with salt, pepper; and a clove or two of garlic. Serve hot or cold to taste.

CALF'S FOOT JELLY, No. 1

After carefully washing one calf's foot, split and put it on with one quart water. Boil from four to five hours. Strain and let stand overnight. Put on stove next day and when it begins to boil add the stiff-beaten whites of two eggs; boil till clear, then strain through cheesecloth. Add sherry and sugar to taste. Let it become firm before serving.

SULZE VON KALBSFUESSEN (CALF'S FOOT JELLY), No. 2

Take one calf's head and four calf's feet, and clean carefully. Let them lay in cold water for half an hour. Set on to boil with four quarts of water. Add two or three small onions, a few cloves, salt, one teaspoon of whole peppers, two or three bay leaves, juice of a large lemon (extract the seeds), one cup of white wine and a little white wine vinegar (just enough to give a tart taste). Let this boil slowly for five or six hours (it must boil until it is reduced one-half). Then strain, through a fine hair sieve and let it stand ten or twelve hours. Remove the meat from the bones and when cold cut into fine pieces. Add also the boiled brains (which must be taken up carefully to avoid falling to pieces). Skim off every particle of fat from the jelly and melt slowly. Add one teaspoon of sugar and the whipped whites of three eggs, and boil very fast for about fifteen minutes, skimming well. Taste, and if not tart enough, add a dash of vinegar. Strain through a flannel bag, do not squeeze or shake it until the jelly ceases to run freely. Remove the bowl and put another under, into which you may press out what remains in the bag (this will not be as clear, but tastes quite as good). Wet your mould, put in the jelly and set in a cool place. In order to have a variety, wet another mould and put in the bits of meat, cut up, and the brains and, lastly, the jelly; set this on ice. It must be thick, so that you can cut it into slices to serve.

ASPIC (SULZ)

Set on to boil two calf's feet, chopped up, one pound of beef and one calf's head with one quart water and one cup of white wine. Add one celery root, three small onions, a bunch of parsley, one dozen whole peppercorns, half a dozen cloves, two bay leaves and a teaspoon of fine salt. Boil steadily for eight hours and then pour through a fine hair sieve. When cold remove every particle of fat and set on to boil again, skimming until clear. Then break two eggs, shells and all, into a deep bowl, beat them up with one cup of vinegar, pour some of the soup stock into this and set all back on the stove to boil up once, stirring all the while. Then remove from the fire and pour through a jelly-bag as you would jelly. Pour into jelly-glasses or one large mould. Set on ice.

GANSLEBER IN SULZ (GOOSE-LIVER ASPIC)

Fry a large goose liver in goose-fat. Season with salt, pepper, a few whole cloves and a very little onion. Cut it up in slices and mix with the sulz and the whites of hard-boiled eggs.

GANSLEBER PURÉE IN SULZ

After the liver is fried, rub it through a sieve or colander and mix with sulz.

GOOSE LIVER

If very large cut in half, dry well on a clean cloth, after having lain in salted water for an hour. Season with fine salt and pepper, fry in very hot goose-fat and add a few cloves. While frying cut up a little onion very fine and add. Then cover closely and smother in this way until you wish to serve. Dredge the liver with flour before frying and turn occasionally. Serve with a slice of lemon on each piece of liver.

GOOSE LIVER WITH GLACÉD CHESTNUTS

Prepare as above and garnish with chestnuts which have been prepared thus: Scald until perfectly white, heat some goose-fat, add nuts, a little sugar and glaze a light brown.

GOOSE LIVER WITH MUSHROOM SAUCE

Take a large white goose liver, lay in salt water for an hour (this rule applies to all kinds of liver), wipe dry, salt, pepper and dredge with flour. Fry in hot goose-fat. Cut up a piece of onion, add a few cloves, a few slices of celery, cut very fine, whole peppers, one bay leaf, and some mushrooms. Cover closely and stew a few minutes. Add lemon juice to sauce.

SPANISH LIVER

Boil in salt water one-half pound calf's liver. Drain and cut into small cubes. Chop one onion, one tablespoon parsley, some mint; add two cloves, a little cinnamon, a little tabasco sauce, one tablespoon olive oil, and one cup of soup stock. Add one cup of bread crumbs which have been soaked in hot water and then drained. Mix all with the liver and bring to a boil. Serve with Spanish rice.

STEWED MILT

Clean the milt thoroughly and boil with your soup meat. Set to boil with cold water and let it boil about two hours. Then take it out and cut into finger lengths and prepare the following sauce: Heat one tablespoon of drippings in a spider. When hot cut up a clove of garlic very fine and brown slightly in the fat. Add a tablespoon of flour, stirring briskly, pepper and salt to taste and thin with soup stock, then the pieces of milt and let it simmer slowly. If the sauce is too thick add more water or soup stock. Some add a few caraway seeds instead of the garlic, which is a matter of taste.

GEFILLTE MILZ (MILT)

Clean the milt by taking off the thin outer skin and every particle of fat that adheres to it. Lay it on a clean board, make an incision with a knife through the centre of the milt, taking care not to cut through the lower skin, and scrape with the edge of a spoon, taking out all the flesh you can without tearing the milt and put it into a bowl until wanted. In the meantime dry the bread, which you have previously soaked in water, in a spider in which you have heated some suet or goose oil, and cut up part of an onion in it very fine. When the bread is thoroughly dried, add it to the flesh scraped from the milt. Also two eggs, one-half teaspoon of salt, pepper, nutmeg and a very little thyme (leave out the latter if you object to the flavor), and add a speck of ground ginger instead. Now work all thoroughly with your hands and fill in the milt. The way to do this is to fill it lengthwise all through the centre and sew it up; when done prick it with a fork in several places to prevent its bursting while boiling. You can parboil it after it is filled in the soup you are to have for dinner, then take it up carefully and brown slightly in a spider of heated fat; or form the mixture into a huge ball and bake it in the oven with flakes of fat put here and there, basting often. Bake until a hard crust is formed over it.

CALF'S LIVER SMOTHERED IN ONIONS

Heat some goose fat in a stew-pan with a close-fitting lid. Cut up an onion in it and when the onion is of a light yellow color, place in the liver which you have previously sprinkled with fine salt and dredged with flour. Add a bay leaf, five cloves and two peppercorns. Cover up tight and stew the liver, turning it occasionally and when required adding a little hot water.

CHICKEN LIVERS

Slice three or four livers from chicken or other fowl and dredge well with flour. Fry one minced onion in one tablespoon of fat until light brown. Put in the liver and shake the pan over the fire to sear all sides. Add one-half teaspoon of salt, one-eighth teaspoon of paprika and one-half cup of strong soup stock. Allow it to boil up once. Add one tablespoon claret or sherry and serve immediately on toast.

KISCHKES—RUSSIAN STYLE

Buy beef casings of butcher. Make a filling of fat, flour (using one-third cup fat to one cup flour) and chopped onions. Season well with salt and pepper, cut them in short lengths, fasten one end, stuff and then fasten the open end. If they are not already cleaned the surface exposed after filling the casing is scraped until cleaned after having been plunged into boiling water. Slice two large onions in a roasting-pan, and roast the kischkes slowly until well done and well browned. Baste frequently with liquid in the pan.

KISCHKES

Prepare as above. If the large casings are used they need not be cut in shorter lengths. Boil for three hours in plenty of water and when done, put in frying-pan with one tablespoon of fat, cover and let brown nicely. Serve hot.

HASHED CALF'S LUNG AND HEART

Lay the lung and heart in water for half an hour and then put on to boil in a soup kettle with your soap meat intended for dinner. When soft, remove from the soup and chop up quite fine. Heat one tablespoon of goose fat in a spider; chop up an onion very fine and add to the heated fat. When yellow, add the hashed lung and heart, salt, pepper, soup stock and thicken with flour. You may prepare this sweet and sour by adding a little vinegar and brown sugar, one-half teaspoon of cinnamon and one tablespoon of molasses; boil slowly; keep covered until ready to serve.

TRIPE À LA CREOLE

Boil tripe with onion, parsley, celery, and seasoning; cut in small pieces, then boil up in the following sauce: Take one tablespoon of fat, brown it with two tablespoons of flour; then add one can of boiled and strained tomatoes, one can of mushrooms, salt and pepper to taste. Serve in ramekins.

TRIPE, FAMILY STYLE

Scald and scrape two pounds tripe and cut into inch squares. Take big kitchen spoon of drippings and put in four large onions quartered and three small cloves of garlic cut up very fine. Let steam, but not brown. When onions begin to cook, put in tripe and steam half an hour. Then cover tripe with water and let cook slowly three hours. Boil a few potatoes and cut in dice shapes and add to it. Half an hour before serving, add the following, after taking off as much fat from the tripe as possible: Three tablespoons of flour thinned with little water; add catsup, paprika, ginger, and one teaspoon of salt. It should all be quite thick, like paste, when cooked.

BOILED TONGUE, (SWEET AND SOUR)

Lay the fresh tongue in cold water for a couple of hours and then put it on to boil in enough water to barely cover it, adding salt. Boil until tender. To ascertain when tender run a fork through the thickest part. A good rule is to boil it, closely covered, from three to four hours steadily. Pare off the thick skin which covers the tongue, cut into even slices, sprinkle a little fine salt over each piece and then prepare the following sauce: Put one tablespoon of drippings in a kettle or spider (goose fat is very good). Cut up an onion in it, add a tablespoon of flour and stir, adding gradually about a pint of the liquor in which the tongue was boiled. Cut up a lemon in slices, remove the seeds, and add two dozen raisins, a few pounded almonds, a stick of cinnamon and a few cloves. Sweeten with four tablespoons of brown sugar in which you have put one-half teaspoon of ground cinnamon, one tablespoon of molasses and two tablespoons of vinegar. Let this boil, lay in the slices of tongue and boil up for a few minutes.

FILLED TONGUE

Take a pickled tongue, cut it open; chop or grind some corned beef; add one egg; brown a little onion, and add some soaked bread; fill tongue with it, and sew it up and boil until done.

SMOKED TONGUE

Put on to boil in a large kettle, fill with cold water, enough to completely cover the tongue; keep adding hot water as it boils down so as to keep it covered with water until done. Keep covered with a lid while boiling and put a heavy weight on the top of the lid so as not to let the steam escape. (If you have an old flat iron use it as a weight.) It should boil very slowly and steadily for four hours. When tongue is cooked set it outdoors to cool in the liquor in which it was boiled. If the tongue is very dry, soak overnight before boiling. In serving slice very thin and garnish with parsley.

SMOTHERED TONGUE

Scald tongue, and then skin. Season well with salt and pepper and slice an onion over it. Let it stand overnight. Put some drippings in a covered iron pot, and then the tongue, with whatever juice the seasoning drew. Cover closely and let it cook slowly until tender—about three hours.

PICKLED BEEF TONGUE

Select a large, fresh beef tongue. Soak in cold water one-half hour. Crush a piece of saltpetre, size of walnut, one teacup of salt, one teaspoon of pepper, three small cloves of garlic cut fine; mix seasoning. Drain water off tongue. With a pointed knife prick tongue; rub in seasoning. Put tongue in crock; add the balance of salt, etc.; cover with plate and weight. Allow to stand from four to five days. Without washing off the seasoning, boil in fresh water until tender.

MEATS

The majority of the cuts of meat which are kosher are those which require long, slow cooking. These cuts of meat are the most nutritious ones and by long, slow cooking can be made as acceptable as the more expensive cuts of meat; they are best boiled or braised.

In order to shut in the juices the meat should at first be subjected to a high degree of heat for a short time. A crust or case will then be formed on the outside, after which the heat should be lowered and the cooking proceed slowly.

This rule holds good for baking, where the oven must be very hot for the first few minutes only; for boiling, where the water must be boiling and covered for a time, and then placed where it will simmer only; for broiling, where the meat must be placed close to the red-hot coals or under the broiler flame of the gas stove at first, then held farther away.

Do not pierce the meat with a fork while cooking, as it makes an outlet for the juices. If necessary, to turn it, use two spoons.

PAN ROAST BEEF

Take a piece of cross-rib or shoulder, about two and one-half to three pounds, put in a small frying-pan with very little fat; have the pan very hot, let the meat brown on all sides, turning it continually until all sides are done, which will require thirty minutes altogether. Lift the meat out of pan to a hot platter, brown some onions, serve these with the meat.

AN EASY POT ROAST

Take four pounds of brisket, season with salt, pepper and ginger, add three tablespoons of tomatoes and an onion cut up. Cover with water in an iron pot and a close-fitting cover, put in oven and bake from three to four hours.

POT ROAST. BRAISED BEEF

Heat some fat or goose fat in a deep iron pot, cut half an onion very fine and when it is slightly browned put in the meat. Cover up closely and let the meat brown on all sides. Salt to taste, add a scant half teaspoon of paprika, half a cup of hot water and simmer an hour longer, keeping covered closely all the time. Add one-half a sweet green pepper (seeds removed), one small carrot cut in slices, two tablespoons of tomatoes and two onions sliced.

Two and a half pounds of brisket shoulder or any other meat suitable for pot roasting will require three hours slow cooking. Shoulder of lamb may also be cooked in this style.

When the meat is tender, remove to a warm platter, strain the gravy, rubbing the thick part through the sieve and after removing any fat serve in a sauce boat.

If any meat is left over it can be sliced and warmed over in the gravy, but the gravy must be warmed first and the meat cook for a short time only as it is already done enough and too much cooking will render it tasteless.

BRISKET OF BEEF (BRUSTDECKEL)

If the brisket has been used for soup, take it out of the soup when it is tender and prepare it with a horseradish sauce, garlic sauce or onion sauce. (See "Sauces for Meats".)

BRISKET OF BEEF WITH SAUERKRAUT

Take about three pounds of fat, young beef (you may make soup stock of it first), then take out the bones, salt it well and lay it in the bottom of a kettle, put a quart of sauerkraut on top of it and let it boil slowly until tender. Add vinegar if necessary, thicken with a grated raw potato and add a little brown sugar. Some like a few caraway seeds added.

SAUERBRATEN

Take a piece of cross-rib or middle cut of chuck about three pounds, and put it in a deep earthen jar and pour enough boiling vinegar over it to cover; you may take one-third water. Add to the vinegar when boiling four bay leaves, some whole peppercorns, cloves and whole mace. Pour this over the meat and turn it daily. In summer three days is the longest time allowed for the meat to remain in this pickle; but in winter eight days is not too long. When ready to boil, heat one tablespoon drippings in a stew-pan. Cut up one or two onions in it; stew until tender and then put in the beef, salting it on both sides before stewing. Stew closely covered and if not acid enough add some of the brine in which it was pickled. Stew about three hours and thicken the gravy with flour.

ROLLED BEEF—POT-ROASTED

Take one pound and one-half of tenderloin, sprinkle it with parsley and onion; season with pepper and salt; roll and tie it. Place it in a pan with soup stock (or water if you have no stock), carrot and bay leaf and pot roast for one and one-half hours. Serve with tomato or brown sauce.

MOCK DUCK

Take the tenderloin, lay it flat on a board after removing the fat. Make a stuffing as for poultry. See "To Stuff Poultry". Spread this mixture on the meat evenly; then roll and tie it with white twine; turn in the ends to make it even and shapely.

Cut into dice an onion, turnip, and carrot, and place them in a baking-pan; lay the rolled meat on the bed of vegetables; pour in enough stock or water to cover the pan one inch deep; add a bouquet made of parsley, one bay leaf and three cloves; cover with another pan, and let cook slowly for four hours, basting frequently. It can be done in a pot just as well, and should be covered as tight as possible; when cooked, strain off the vegetables; thicken the gravy with one tablespoon of flour browned in fat and serve it with the meat. Long, slow cooking is required to make the meat tender. If cooked too fast it will not be good.

MARROWBONES

Have the bones cut into pieces two or three inches long; scrape and wash them very clean; spread a little thick dough on each end to keep the marrow in; then tie each bone in a piece of cloth and boil them for one hour. Remove the cloth and paste, and place each bone on a square of toast; sprinkle with red pepper and serve very hot. Or the marrow-bone can be boiled without being cut, the marrow then removed with a spoon and placed on squares of hot toast. Serve for luncheon.

ROAST BEEF, No. 1

Take prime rib roast. Cut up a small onion, a celery root and part of a carrot into rather small pieces and add to these two or three sprigs of parsley and one bay leaf. Sprinkle these over the bottom of the dripping-pan and place your roast on this bed. The oven should be very hot when the roast is first put in, but when the roast is browned sufficiently to retain its juices, moderate the heat and roast more slowly until the meat is done. Do not season until the roast is browned, and then add salt and pepper. Enough juice and fat will drop from the roast to give the necessary broth for basting. Baste frequently and turn occasionally, being very careful, however, not to stick a fork into the roast.

ROAST BEEF, No. 2

Season meat with salt and paprika. Dredge with flour. Place on rack in dripping-pan with two or three tablespoons fat, in hot oven, to brown quickly. Reduce heat and baste every ten minutes with the fat that has fried out. When meat is about half done, turn it over, dredge with flour, finish browning. If necessary, add a small quantity of water. Allow fifteen to twenty minutes for each pound of meat.

Three pounds is the smallest roast practicable.

ROAST BEEF (RUSSIAN STYLE)

Place a piece of cross-rib or shoulder weighing three pounds in roasting-pan, slice some onions over it, season with salt and pepper, add some water and let it cook well. Then peel a few potatoes and put them under the meat. When the meat becomes brown, turn it and cook until it browns on the other side.

WIENER BRATEN—VIENNA ROAST

Take a shoulder, have the bone taken out and then pound the meat well with a mallet. Lay it in vinegar for twenty-four hours. Heat some fat or goose oil in a deep pan or kettle which has a cover that fits air tight and lay the meat in the hot fat and sprinkle the upper side with salt, pepper and ginger. Put an onion in with the meat; stick about half a dozen cloves in the onion and add one bay leaf. Now turn the meat over and sprinkle the other side with salt, pepper and ginger. Cut up one or two tomatoes and pour some soup stock over all, and a dash of white wine. Cover closely and stew very slowly for three or four hours, turning the meat now and then; in doing so do not pierce with the fork, as this will allow the juice to escape. Do not add any water. Make enough potato pancakes to serve one or two to each person with "Wiener Braten."

TO BROIL STEAK BY GAS

Wipe steak with a damp cloth. Trim off the surplus fat. When the oven has been heated for from five to seven minutes, lay steak on a rack, greased, as near the flame as possible, the position of the rack depending on the thickness of the steak. Let the steak sear on each side, thereby retaining the juice. Then lower the rack somewhat, and allow the steak to broil to the degree required. Just before taking from the oven, salt and pepper and spread with melted chicken fat.

You can get just as good results in preparing chops and fish in the broiling oven.

BROILED BEEFSTEAK

Heat the gridiron, put in the steak, turn the gridiron over the hot coals at intervals of two minutes and then repeatedly at intervals of one minute. Sprinkle with salt and pepper, and serve on a hot platter.

Chops are done in the same way, but the gridiron is turned twice at intervals of two minutes and six times at intervals of one minute.

FRIED STEAK WITH ONIONS

Season the steak with salt and pepper, and dredge with flour. If tough, chop on both sides with a sharp knife. Lay in a pan of hot fat, when brown on one side, turn and brown on the other. While the steak is frying, heat some fat in another fryer and drop in four of five white onions that have been cut up. Fry crisp but not black. Remove the steak to a hot platter, stir one tablespoon of flour in the fryer until smooth, add one-half cup of boiling water. Lay the crisp onions over the steak, then over all pour the brown gravy.

FRIED BEEFSTEAK

Take third cut of chuck or the tenderloin. Have the spider very hot, use just enough fat to grease the spider. Lay in the steak, turning very often to keep in the juice, season with salt and pepper. Serve on a hot platter.

BRUNSWICK STEW

Cook one pound of brisket of beef and three pounds of young chicken with one pint of soup stock or water, one pint of Lima beans, four ears of cut corn (cut from cob), three potatoes diced, two tomatoes quartered; one small onion, one teaspoon of paprika and one teaspoon of salt. Let all these simmer until tender, and before serving remove the meat and any visible chicken bones.

This stew may be made of breast of veal omitting the chicken and brisket.

BREAST FLANK (SHORT RIBS) AND YELLOW TURNIPS

Get the small ribs and put on with plenty of water, an onion, pepper and salt. After boiling about one and one-half hours add a large yellow turnip cut in small pieces; one-half hour before serving add six potatoes cut in small pieces. Water must be added as necessary. A little sugar will improve flavor, and as it simmers the turnip will soften and give the whole dish the appearance of a stew.

MEAT OLIVES

Have a flank steak cut in three inch squares. Spread each piece with the following dressing: one cup of bread crumbs, two tablespoons of minced parsley; one chopped onion, a dash of red pepper and one teaspoon of salt. Moisten with one-fourth cup of melted fat. Roll up and tie in shape. Cover with water and simmer until meat is tender. Take the olives from the sauce and brown in the oven. Thicken the sauce with one-fourth cup of flour moistened with water to form a thin paste.

SHORT RIB OF BEEF, SPANISH

Get the small ribs of beef and put on with water enough to cover, seasoning with salt, pepper, an onion and a tiny clove of garlic. Let it cook about two hours, then add a can of tomatoes and season highly either with red peppers or paprika. Cook at least three hours.

BRAISED OXTAILS

Two oxtails, jointed and washed; six onions sliced and browned in pot with oxtails. When nicely browned add water enough to cover and stew slowly one hour; then add two carrots, if small; one green pepper, sprig of parsley, one-half cup of tomatoes and six small potatoes, and cook until tender. Thicken with browned flour. Cook separately eight lengths of macaroni; place cooked macaroni on dish and pour ragout over it and serve hot.

To brown flour take one-half cup of flour, put in pan over moderate heat and stir until nicely browned.

HUNGARIAN GOULASH

Have two pounds of beef cut into one inch squares. Dredge in flour and fry until brown. Cover with water and simmer for two hours; the last half-hour add one tablespoon of salt and one-eighth of a teaspoon of pepper. Make a sauce by cooking one cup of tomatoes and one stalk of celery cut in small pieces, a bay leaf and two whole cloves, for twenty-five minutes; rub through a sieve, add to stock in which meat was cooked. Thicken with four tablespoons of flour moistened with two tablespoons of water. Serve meat with cooked diced potatoes, carrots, and green and red peppers cut in strips.

RUSSIAN GOULASH

To one pound beef, free from fat and cut up as pan stew, add one chopped green pepper, one large onion, two blades of garlic (cut fine), pepper and salt, with just enough water to cover. Let this simmer until meat is very tender. Add a little water as needed. Put in medium sized can of tomatoes an hour or so before using and have ready two cups of cooked spaghetti or macaroni and put this into the meat until thoroughly heated. This must not be too wet; let water cook away just before adding the tomatoes.

BEEF LOAF

To two pounds of chopped beef take three egg yolks, three tablespoons of parsley, three tablespoons of melted chicken-fat, four heaping tablespoons of soft bread crumbs, one-half teaspoon of kitchen bouquet, two teaspoons of lemon juice, grated peel of one lemon, one teaspoon of salt, one-half teaspoon of onion-juice and one teaspoon of pepper. Mix and bake twenty-five minutes in a quick oven with one-fourth cup of melted chicken-fat, and one-half cup of boiling water. Baste often.

HAMBURGER STEAK

Take one pound of raw beef, cut off fat and stringy pieces, chop extremely fine, season with salt and pepper, grate in part of an onion or fry with onions. Make into round cakes a little less than one-half inch thick. Heat pan blue hot, grease lightly; add cakes, count sixty, then turn them and cook on the other side until brown. When well browned they are done if liked rare. Cook ten minutes if liked well done.

BITKI (RUSSIAN HAMBURGER STEAK)

Take two cups of clear beef chopped, and two cups of bread crumbs that have been soaked in a little water, leaving them quite moist, mix thoroughly with the beef, season with pepper and salt and shape into individual cakes. Fry as directed for Hamburger Steak.

CHOPPED MEAT WITH RAISINS (ROUMANIAN)

Take a pound of chopped meat, add grated onion, an egg, matzoth flour, white pepper, mix and form into small balls, put in pot with one-half cup of water, fat, sugar, a quarter cup of large black raisins, a few slices of lemon and let stew one-half hour, then thicken gravy with tablespoon of flour browned in a tablespoon of fat and serve.

CARNATZLICH (ROUMANIAN)

One pound of tenderloin, chopped, add an egg, a little paprika, black pepper, salt and four cloves of garlic (which have been scraped, and let stand in a little salt for ten minutes, and then mashed so it looks like dough). Form this meat mixture into short sausage-like rolls; boil one-half hour and serve at once.

Serve this dish with Slaitta. (See Vegetables.)

BAKED HASH

Mix together one cup of chopped meat, one cup of cold mashed potatoes, one-half an onion, minced, one well-beaten egg and one-half cup of soup stock. Season rather highly with salt, if unsalted meat is used, paprika and celery salt, turn into greased baking dish and bake for twenty minutes in a well-heated oven. The same mixture may be fried, but will not taste as good.

SOUP MEAT

The meat must be cooked until very tender then lift it out of the soup and lay upon a platter and season while hot. Heat a tablespoon of fat or drippings of roast beef in a spider, cut up a few slices of onion in it, also half a clove of garlic, add a tablespoon of flour, stirring all the time; then add soup stock or rich gravy, and the soup meat, which has been seasoned with salt, pepper and ginger. You must sprinkle the spices on both sides of the meat, and add one-half teaspoon of caraway seed to the sauce, and if too thick add more soup stock and a little boiling water. Cover closely and let it simmer about fifteen minutes.

LEFT-OVER MEAT

There are many ways to utilize left-over meat.

Indeed, not one particle of meat should ever be wasted.

Cold roasts of beef, lamb, mutton or any cold joint roasted or boiled may be made into soups, stews, minces or used for sandwiches, or just served cold with vegetables or salads.

SPAGHETTI AND MEAT

Break spaghetti in small pieces and boil until tender. Put left-over meat through chopper and mix with the spaghetti, salt, pepper, and a little onion juice. Grease a baking dish and put in the meat and spaghetti, sprinkle on top with bread crumbs and bake in a moderate oven.

MEAT PIE

Cut any left-over beef, lamb or veal in small pieces, removing all excess of fat; parboil one green pepper (seeds removed) cut in strips, two cups of potatoes and one-half cup of carrots cut in dice, and one onion chopped fine. Add to the meat. Thicken with one-fourth cup of flour moistened in cold water. Put in a baking dish. The crust is made as follows: One cup of flour, one heaping teaspoon of drippings, pinch of salt, one-fourth teaspoon of baking powder, one teaspoon of sugar and cold water to mix, about one-third cup. Roll out to fit baking dish, cut holes for steam to escape, after covering the contents of the dish. Bake in a quick hot oven one-half hour.

PICKLED MEAT—HOME-MADE CORNED BEEF

Take four quarts of water, adding enough salt to float an egg, boil this salted water, when cool take four or five pounds brisket of beef, seasoned with whole and ground peppers, one large clove of garlic, pierced in different parts of the beef, one tablespoon of sugar, one bay leaf and one teaspoon of saltpetre. Put meat into deep stone pot, pour the boiled water over it and store in a cool place for ten days or two weeks.

BOILED CORNED BEEF

Put corned beef into cold water; using enough to cover it well; let it come slowly to the boiling-point; then place where it will simmer only; allow thirty minutes or more to each pound. It is improved by adding a few soup vegetables the last hour of cooking.

If the piece can be used a second time, trim it to good shape; place it again in the water in which it was boiled; let it get heated through; then set aside to cool in the water, and under pressure, a plate or deep dish holding a flat-iron being set on top of the meat. The water need not rise above the meat sufficiently to wet the iron. When cooled under pressure the meat is more firm and cuts better into slices.

Cabbage is usually served with hot corned beef, but should not be boiled with it.

ENCHILADAS

Make a dough of cornmeal and wheat flour and water. Roll it out in thin, round cakes; cook quickly in a pan that has not been greased, then roll in a cloth to keep soft and warm. Grind one cup of sausage, add one-half grated onion, one tablespoon of Worcestershire sauce, and fill the warm cakes with this mixture. Roll them when filled, and pour over them a sauce made of two tablespoons of drippings into which two tablespoons of flour have been smoothed. Add one cup of soup stock, one cup of strained tomatoes, two tablespoons of vinegar, one tablespoon of Spanish pepper sauce.

VIENNA SAUSAGE

Wash and put on in boiling water. Boil ten minutes, fill a deep dish with hot water, put sausages in, cover, and serve in hot water. To be eaten with grated horseradish or French mustard.

SMOKED BEEF

Soak overnight in cold water; next morning place it in cold water, and simmer till quite tender, reckoning one-half hour to the pound.

ROAST VEAL

The shoulder and breast of veal are best for roasting. Always buy veal that is fat and white. Prepare for the oven in the following manner: Wash and then dry; rub it well with salt, a very little ground ginger, and dredge it well with flour. Lay in roasting-pan and put slices of onion on top with a few tablespoons of goose-fat or drippings. Cover tightly and roast, allowing twenty minutes to the pound and baste frequently. Veal must be well done. When cold it slices up as nicely as turkey.

BREAST OF VEAL—ROASTED

Roast as directed above. Have the butcher cut a pocket to receive the stuffing. Prepare bread stuffing and sew up the pocket. Sprinkle a little caraway seed on top of the roast. A tablespoon of lemon juice adds to the flavor. Baste often.

STEWED VEAL

Prepare as above, but do not have the meat cut in small pieces. If desired one-half teaspoon of caraway seed may be used instead of the parsley. Mashed potatoes and green peas or stewed tomatoes are usually served with veal.

Any of the flour or potato dumplings are excellent served with stewed or fricasseed veal.

FRICASSEED VEAL WITH CAULIFLOWER

Use the breast or shoulder for this purpose, the former being preferable, and cut it up into pieces, not too small. Sprinkle each piece slightly with fine salt and ginger. Heat a tablespoon of goose-oil or poultry drippings in a stew-pan, and lay the veal in it. Cut up an onion and one or two tomatoes (a tablespoon of canned tomatoes will do), and add to this a little water, and stew two hours, closely covered. When done mix a teaspoon of flour and a little water and add to the veal. Chop up a few sprigs of parsley, add it and boil up once and serve. Place the cauliflower around the platter in which you serve the veal. Boil the cauliflower in salt and water, closely covered.

STUFFED SHOULDER OF VEAL

Have the blade removed, and fill the space with a stuffing made of bread crumbs, thyme, lemon juice, salt, pepper to taste and one egg, also chopped mushrooms if desired. Sew up the opening, press and tie it into good shape and roast. The stuffing may be made of minced meat, cut from the veal, and highly seasoned.

VEAL LOAF

Take two pounds of chopped veal, four tablespoons of bread crumbs, two beaten eggs, season with salt, pepper, ginger, nutmeg and a little water. Add a tablespoon of chicken-fat; grease the pan, mix ingredients thoroughly, form into a loaf, spread or lay piece of chicken-fat on top. Bake in oblong tin until done, basting frequently.

POULTRY

TO DRESS AND CLEAN POULTRY

Singe by holding the fowl over a flame from gas, alcohol or burning paper. Pick off pin feathers. Cut off the nails, then cut off the head, turn back the skin and cut the neck off quite close; take out windpipe and crop, cutting off close to the body. Cut through the skin around the leg one inch below the leg joint; take out the tendons and break the leg at the joint; in old birds each tendon must be removed separately by using a skewer.

Make an incision just below the breast bone large enough to insert your hand, take out the fat and loosen the entrails with your forefinger. When everything is removed, cut off the wings close to the body, also the neck, feet and head. Separate the gall from the liver. In doing this be very careful not to break the gall, which has a very thin skin. Scrape all the fat off carefully that adheres to the entrails and lay it in a separate dish of water overnight. Cut open the gizzard, clean and pull off the skin, or inner lining.

Make Kosher as directed in "Rules for Kashering".

If you make use of the head, which you may in soup, cut off the top of the bill, split open the head, lengthwise, take out the brains, eyes and tongue.

Clean the gizzard and feet by laying them in scalding water for a few moments, this will loosen the skin, which can then be easily removed.

Remove the oil bag from the upper side of tail.

After making Kosher and cleaning poultry, season all fowls for several hours before cooking. Salt, pepper, and ginger are the proper seasoning. Some like a tiny bit of garlic rubbed inside and outside, especially for goose or duck.

Dress and clean goose, duck, squab, and turkey as directed for chicken.

TO TRUSS A CHICKEN

Press the thighs and wings close against the body; fasten securely with skewers and tie with string. Draw the skin of the neck to the back and fasten it.

ROAST CHICKEN

Stuff and truss a chicken, season with pepper and salt and dredge with flour. Put in a roasting-pan with two or three tablespoons of chicken-fat if the chicken is not especially fat. When heated add hot water and baste frequently. The oven should be hot and the time necessary for a large chicken will be about an hour and a half. When done, remove the chicken, pour off the grease and make a brown sauce in the pan.

CHICKEN CASSEROLE

Bake chicken in covered casserole until nearly tender, then add three potatoes cut in dice; boil small pieces of carrots, green peas, and small white onions—each to be boiled separately. Just before serving, thicken gravy with a teaspoon of flour mixed with a half cup of soup stock or water. Season to taste and place vegetables around the dish.

BOILED CHICKEN, BAKED

Make chicken soup with an old hen. Remove chicken from soup just as soon as tender. Place in roasting-pan with three tablespoons of chicken-fat, one onion sliced, one clove of garlic, one-half teaspoon each of salt and paprika. Sprinkle with soft bread crumbs. Baste frequently and when sufficiently browned, cut in pieces for serving. Place on platter with the strained gravy pour over the chicken and serve.

BROILED SPRING CHICKEN

Take young spring chickens of one to one and one-half pounds in weight, and split down the back, break the joints and remove the breast bone. Sprinkle with salt and pepper and rub well with chicken-fat. Place in broiler and broil twenty minutes over a clear fire, or under the flame in broiling oven of gas stove, being careful to turn broiler that all parts may be equally browned. The flesh side must be exposed to the fire the greater part of the time as the skin side will brown quickly. Remove to hot platter.

Or chicken may be placed in dripping pan, skin side down, seasoned with salt and pepper and spread with chicken-fat, and bake fifteen minutes in a hot oven and then broiled to finish.

Serve with giblet sauce.

FRIED SPRING CHICKEN

Cut it up as for fricassee and see that every piece is wiped dry. Have ready heated in a spider some goose-fat or other poultry drippings. Season each piece of chicken with salt and ground ginger, or pepper. Roll each piece of chicken in sifted cracker or bread crumbs (which you have previously seasoned with salt). Fry in the spider, turning often, and browning evenly. You may cut up some parsley and add while frying. If the chicken is quite large, it is better to steam it before frying.

GIBLETS

Heart, liver and gizzard constitute the giblets, and to these the neck is usually added. Wash them; put them in cold water and cook until tender. This will take several hours. Serve with the chicken; or mash the liver, mince the heart and gizzard and add them to the brown sauce. Save the stock in which they are cooked for making the sauce.

CHICKEN FRICASSEE

Take a chicken, cut off the wings, legs and neck. Separate the breast from the chicken, leaving it whole. Cut the back into two pieces. Prepare a mixture of salt, ginger and a little pepper in a saucer and dust each piece of chicken with this mixture. When you are ready to cook the chicken, take all the particles of fat you have removed from it and lay in the bottom of the kettle, also a small onion, cut up, some parsley root and celery. Lay the chicken upon this, breast first, then the leg and so on. Cover up tight and let it stew slowly on the back of the stove (or over a low gas flame), adding hot water when necessary. Just before serving chop up some parsley, fine, and rub a teaspoon of flour in a little cold water, and add. Let it boil up once. Shake the kettle back and forth to prevent becoming lumpy. The parsley root and celery may be omitted if so desired.

Duck can be prepared in this manner.

CHICKEN WITH RICE

Joint a chicken; season with salt and ground ginger and boil with water enough to cover. Allow one-half pound of rice to one chicken. Boil this after chicken is tender. Serve together on a large platter.

CHICKEN (TURKISH STYLE)

Brown a chicken, cover with water and season, cook until tender. When chicken is tender; slash the skin of chestnuts, put them in oven and roast, then skin them, put in chicken and let come to a boil and serve with the chicken.

AMASTICH

Cook one pound of rice in a quart of stock for half an hour, stirring frequently. Then add a chicken stuffed and trussed as for roasting; cover closely and cook thoroughly. After removing the chicken, pass the liquor through a strainer, add the juice of a lemon and the beaten yolk of an egg, and pour over the bird.

CHICKEN WITH SPAGHETTI EN CASSEROLE

Prepare and truss a young chicken, as if for roasting. Put it in a casserole; and pour over it two tablespoons of olive oil, a cup of white wine, a cup of bouillon, salt and cayenne to taste, one spoon of dried mushrooms soaked in one cup of water and chopped fine, and one-half can of mushrooms. Cover tightly and simmer in the oven for about an hour, turning the chicken occasionally; add a dozen olives and a tablespoon of chicken-fat, smoothed with one tablespoon of flour, and bring to a boil. Remove the chicken and add about a pint of boiled spaghetti to the sauce. Place the chicken on a platter, surround with the spaghetti, and serve.

STUFFED CHICKEN (TURKISH STYLE)

Steam chicken and when it is almost tender stuff it with the following: Take one-fourth pound of almonds, chopped; season with parsley, pepper and salt to taste, add one tablespoon of bread crumbs and bind this with one well-beaten egg. Put chicken in roasting-pan and roast until done.

SMOTHERED CHICKEN

Two tender chickens cut in half, split down the back; place the pieces in a colander to drain well, after having been well salted; season with pepper; grease well the bottom of a baking-pan; add one stalk finely chopped celery, onion; lay the chicken on breast, side up; sprinkle lightly with flour, fat; two cups of hot water. Have the oven very hot when putting chickens in. As soon as browned evenly, cover with a pan, fitting closely. Reduce the heat of the oven; allow to cook slowly an hour or so longer, until tender. Place on a hot platter; set in oven until sauce is made, as follows: put the pan on top of stove in which chickens were smothered; add level tablespoon of flour, thinned in cold water; add minced parsley; let this all cook two or three minutes, then add large cup of strong stock, to the chickens. Broil one can mushrooms, and pour these over chicken when ready to serve.

CHICKEN CURRY

Cut chickens in pieces for serving; dredge in flour and sauté in hot fat. Cut one onion in thin pieces, add one tablespoon of curry powder, three-fourths of a tablespoon of salt and one tablespoon of wine vinegar. Add to chicken, cover with boiling water; simmer until chicken is tender. Thicken sauce and serve with steamed rice.

CHICKEN PAPRIKA WITH RICE

Cut a three and one-half pound fat chicken in pieces to serve, salt it and let stand several hours. Heat one-fourth cup of fat in an iron kettle, add one medium-sized onion, minced; fry golden brown and set aside. Fry the chicken in the fat and when nicely browned, add paprika to taste and boiling water to cover, and let simmer one hour.

Soak one cup of rice in cold water, drain, add the fried onion and one teaspoon of salt and gradually three cups of chicken broth, more if necessary. When nearly done add the chicken and finish cooking in a slow oven, one-half hour.

CHILI CON CARNE

Cut two broilers in pieces for serving. Season with salt, pepper, and dredge in flour; brown in hot fat. Parboil six large red peppers until soft, rub through a wire sieve. Chop two small onions fine, three cloves of garlic and one-fourth cup of capers. Combine, add to chicken, cover with water and cook until chicken is tender. Thicken the sauce with fat and flour melted together.

PILAF (RUSSIAN STYLE)

Follow recipe below but substitute cooked lamb for the chicken, and add chicken livers fried and cut in small pieces.

PILAF (TURKISH STYLE)

Soak one cup of rice in cold water for one hour. Pour off the water, and put the rice with two cups of soup stock and one-quarter of a white onion on to boil. Stew until the rice absorbs all the stock. Stew one-half can of tomatoes thoroughly and season with olive oil or chicken-fat, salt and pepper. Mix it with the rice.

Sauté in chicken-fat to a light color, a jointed chicken slightly parboiled, or slices of cold cooked chicken or turkey. Make a depression in the rice and tomato, put in the chicken and two tablespoons of olive oil or chicken-fat, and stew all together for twenty minutes. Serve on a platter in a smooth mound, the red rice surrounding the fowl.

SPANISH PIE

Take one pint of cold chicken, duck or any poultry. Cut it into flakes and place it in a pudding dish which has been lined with a thin crust. On the layer of meat place a layer of sweet red peppers (seeds removed), cut in slices; next, a layer of thinly sliced sausage, and so on until the dish is full. Over this pour a glass of claret into which have been rubbed two tablespoons of flour. Cover with a thin crust of pastry, and bake.

CHICKEN À LA ITALIENNE

Cut the remains of cold chicken (or turkey) into pieces about an inch long and marinate them in a bowl containing one tablespoon of olive oil; one teaspoon of tarragon vinegar or lemon juice, a few drops of onion juice, salt and pepper. At the end of half an hour sprinkle with finely chopped parsley, dip them in fritter batter, and fry in boiling fat. Drain on a brown paper, and serve with or without tomato or brown sauce.

In some parts of Italy this dish is made of several kinds of cold meats, poultry, brains, etc. (the greater the variety the better), served on the same platter, and in Spain all kinds of cold vegetables are fried in batter and served together.

ROAST GOOSE

All goose meat tastes better if it is well rubbed with salt, ginger and a little garlic a day previous to using.

Stuff goose with bread dressing, or chestnut dressing, a dressing of apples is also very good. (See "Stuffings for Meat and Poultry".) Sew up the goose, then line a sheet-iron roasting-pan with a few slices of onion and celery and place the goose upon these, cover closely, roast three hours or more, according to weight. If the goose browns too quickly, cover with greased paper or lower the heat of the oven. Baste every fifteen minutes.

GESCHUNDENE GANS

Take a very fat goose for this purpose. After cleaning and singeing, cut off neck, wings and feet. Lay the goose on a table, back up, take a sharp knife, make a cut from the neck down to the tai. Begin again at the top near the neck, take off the skin, holding it in your left hand, your knife in your right hand, after all the skin is removed, place it in cold water; separate the breast from back and cut off joints. Have ready in a plate a mixture of salt, ginger and a little garlic or onion, cut up fine. Rub the joints and small pieces with this, and make a small incision in each leg and four in the breast. Put in each incision a small piece of garlic or onion, and rub also with a prepared mixture of salt and ginger. Put away in stone jar overnight or until you wish to use.

GAENSEKLEIN

Rub wings, neck, gizzard, heart and back of goose with salt, ginger, pepper and garlic and set on the fire in a stew-pan with cold water. Cover tightly and stew slowly but steadily for four hours. When done skim off all the fat. Now put a spider over the fire, put into it about two or three tablespoons of the fat that you have just skimmed off and then add the fat to the meat again. Cut up fine a very small piece of garlic and add a heaping teaspoon of flour (brown). Add the hot gravy and pour all over the goose. Cover up tightly and set on back of stove till you wish to serve. You may cook the whole goose in this way after it is cut up.

STUFFED GOOSE NECK (RUSSIAN STYLE)

Remove skin from neck of goose, duck or chicken in one piece. Wash and clean well and stuff with same mixture as for Kischtke. Sew at both ends and roast in hot oven until well browned.

STUFFED GOOSE NECK

Remove the fat skin from the neck of a fat goose, being careful not to put any holes in it. Clean carefully and sew up the smaller end and stuff through larger end with the following:

Grind fine some pieces of raw goose meat (taken from the breast or legs), grind also some soft or "linda fat" a thin piece of garlic, a small piece of onion, when fine add one egg and a little soaked bread, season with salt, pepper, and ginger. When neck is stuffed, sew up larger end, lay it in a pudding-pan, pour a little cold water over it, set in stove and baste from time to time. Let brown until crisp. Eat hot.

GOOSE CRACKLINGS (GRIEBEN)

Cut the thick fat of a fat goose in pieces as big as the palm of your hand, roll together and run a toothpick through each one to fasten. Put a large preserve kettle on top of hot stove, lay in the cracklings, sprinkle a tiny bit of salt over them and pour in a cup or two of cold water; cover closely and let cook not too fast, until water is cooked out. Then add the soft or "linda" fat, keep top off and let all brown nicely. About one to two hours is required to cook them. If you do not wish the scraps of "Greben" brittle, take them out of the fat before they are browned. Place strainer over your fat crock, to catch the clear fat and let greben drain. If greben are too greasy place in baking-pan in oven a few minutes to try out a little more. Serve at lunch with rye bread.

ROAST GOOSE BREASTS

The best way to roast a goose breast is to remove the skin from the neck and sew it over the breast and fasten it with a few stitches under the breast, making an incision with a pointed knife in the breast and joints of the goose, so as to be able to insert a little garlic (or onion) in each incision, also a little salt and ginger. Keep closely covered all the time, so as not to get too brown. They cut up nicely cold for sandwiches.

GOOSE MEAT, PRESERVED IN FAT

If too fat to roast, render the fat of goose, remove and cut the skin into small pieces. The scraps, when brown, shriveled and crisp, are then "Greben," and are served hot or cold. When fat is nearly done or clear, add the breast and legs of goose, previously salted, and boil in the fat until tender and browned. Place meat in crock and pour the clear, hot fat over it to cover. Cool. Cover crock with plate and stone and keep in a cool, dry place. Will keep for months. When ready to serve, take out meat, heat, and drain off fat.

SMOKED GOOSE BREAST

Dried or smoked goose breast must be prepared in the following manner: Take the breast of a fat goose; leave the skin on; rub well with salt, pepper and saltpetre; pack in a stone jar and let it remain pickled thus four or five days. Dry well, cover with gauze and send away to be smoked.

SMOKED GOOSE

Remove skin. Place legs, neck and skin of neck of geschundene goose (fat goose) to one side. Scrape the meat carefully from the bones, neck, back, etc., of the goose, remove all tendons and tissues and chop very fine. Fill this in the skin of the neck and sew up with coarse thread on both ends. Rub the filled neck, the legs and the breast with plenty of garlic (sprinkle with three-eighths pound of salt and one tablespoon of sugar and one teaspoon of saltpetre), and enough water to form a brine. Place the neck, legs and breast in a stone jar, cover with a cloth and put weights on top. Put aside for seven days, turn once in a while. Take out of the brine, cover with gauze and send to the butcher to smoke. When done, serve cold, sliced thin.

STEWED GOOSE, PIQUANTE

Cut up, after being skinned, and stew, seasoning with salt, pepper, a few cloves and a very little lemon peel. When done heat a little goose fat in a frying-pan, brown half a tablespoon of flour, add a little vinegar and the juice of half a lemon.

MINCED GOOSE (HUNGARIAN STYLE)

Take the entire breast of a goose, chop up fine in a chopping bowl; grate in part of an onion, and season with salt, pepper and a tiny piece of garlic. Add some grated stale bread and work in a few eggs. Press this chopped meat back on to the breast bone and roast, basting very often with goose fat.

DUCK

Singe off all the small feathers; cut off neck and wings, which may be used for soup; wash thoroughly and rub well with salt, ginger and a little pepper, inside and out. Now prepare this dressing: Take the liver, gizzard and heart and chop to a powder in chopping bowl. Grate in a little nutmeg, add a piece of celery root and half an onion. Put all this into your chopping bowl. Soak some stale bread, squeeze out all the water and fry in a spider of hot fat. Toss this soaked bread into the bowl; add one egg, salt, pepper and a speck of ginger and mix all thoroughly. Fill the duck with this and sew it up. Lay in the roasting-pan with slices of onions, celery and specks of fat. Put some on top of fowl; roast two hours, covered up tight and baste often. Stick a fork into the skin from time to time so that the fat will try out.

ROAST DUCK

Draw the duck; stuff, truss and roast the same as chicken. Serve with giblet sauce and currant jelly. If small, the duck should be cooked in an hour.

DUCK À LA MODE IN JELLY

One duckling of about five pounds, one calf's foot, eight to ten small onions, as many young carrots, one bunch of parsley. Cook the foot slowly in one quart of water, one teaspoon of salt and a small bay leaf. Put aside when the liquor has been reduced to one-half. In the meanwhile fry the duck and when well browned wipe off the grease, put in another pan, add the calf's foot with its broth, one glass of dry white wine, a tablespoon of brandy, the carrots, parsley and the onions—the latter slightly browned in drippings—pepper and salt to taste and cook slowly under a covered lid for one hour. Cool off for about an hour, take off the grease, bone and skin the duckling and cut the meat into small pieces; arrange nicely with the vegetables in individual earthenware dishes, cover with the stock and put on the ice to harden.

SQUABS, OR NEST PIGEONS

Pick, singe, draw, clean and season them well inside and out, with salt mixed with a little ginger and pepper, and then stuff them with well-seasoned bread dressing. Pack them closely in a deep stew-pan and cover with flakes of goose fat, minced parsley and a little chopped onion. Cover with a lid that fits close and stew gently, adding water when necessary. Do not let them get too brown. They should be a light yellow.

BROILED SQUABS

Squabs are a great delicacy, especially in the convalescent's menu, being peculiarly savory and nourishing. Clean the squabs; lay them in salt water for about ten minutes and then rub dry with a clean towel. Split them down the back and broil over a clear coal fire. Season with salt and pepper; lay them on a heated platter, grease them liberally with goose fat and cover with a deep platter. Toast a piece of bread for each pigeon, removing the crust. Dip the toast in boiling water for an instant. In serving lay a squab upon a piece of toasted bread.

PIGEON PIE

Prepare as many pigeons as you wish to bake in your pie. Salt and pepper, then melt some fat in a stew-pan, and cut up an onion in it. When hot, place in the pigeons and stew until tender. In the meantime line a deep pie plate with a rich paste. Cut up the pigeons, lay them in, with hard-boiled eggs chopped up and minced parsley. Season with salt and pepper. Put flakes of chicken fat rolled in flour here and there, pour over the gravy the pigeons were stewed in, cover with a crust. Bake slowly until done.

SQUAB EN CASSEROLE

Take fowl and brown in a skillet the desired color, then add to this enough water (or soup stock preferred), put it in casserole and add vegetables; add first those that require longest cooking. Use mushrooms, carrots, small potatoes and peas. If you like flavor of sherry wine, add small wine glass; if not, it is just as good. Season well and cook in hot oven not too long, as you want fowl and vegetables to be whole. You may add soup stock if it is too dry after being in oven.

ROAST TURKEY

Singe and clean the turkey the same as chicken. Fill with plain bread stuffing or chestnut stuffing. Tie down the legs and rub entire surface with salt and let stand overnight. Next morning place in large drippings or roasting-pan on rack and spread breast, legs and wings with one-third cup of fat creamed and mixed with one-fourth cup of flour. Dredge bottom of pan with flour. Place in a hot oven and when the flour on the turkey begins to brown, reduce the heat and add two cups of boiling water or the stock in which the giblets are cooking, and baste with one-fourth cup of fat and three-fourths cup of boiling water. When this is all used, baste with the fat in the pan. Baste every fifteen minutes until tender; do not prick with a fork, press with the fingers; if the breast meat and leg are soft to the touch the turkey is done. If the oven is too hot, cover the pan; turn the turkey often, that it may brown nicely. Remove strings and skewers and serve on hot platter. Serve with giblet sauce and cranberry sauce. If the turkey is very large it will require three hours or more, a small one will require only an hour and a half.

STUFFED TURKEY NECK (TURKISH STYLE)

Take neck of turkey, stuff with following: One-quarter pound of almonds or walnuts chopped fine and seasoned with chopped parsley, pepper and salt, put two hard-boiled eggs in the centre of this dressing; stuff neck, sew up the ends and when roasted slice across so as to have a portion of the hard-boiled egg on each slice; place on platter and surround with sprigs of parsley.

STUFFINGS FOR MEAT AND POULTRY

TO STUFF POULTRY

Use enough stuffing to fill the bird but do not pack it tightly or the stuffing will be soggy. Close the small openings with a skewer; sew the larger one with linen thread and a long needle. Remove skewers and strings before serving.

CRUMB DRESSING

Take one tablespoon of chicken fat, mix in two cups of bread crumbs, pinch of salt and pepper, a few drops of onion juice, one tablespoon of chopped parsley, and lastly one well-beaten egg. Mix all on stove in skillet, remove from fire and stuff fowl.

BREAD DRESSING FOR FOWL

In a fryer on the stove heat two tablespoons of drippings or fat, drop in one-half onion cut fine, brown lightly and add one-quarter loaf of stale baker's bread (which has previously been soaked in cold water and then thoroughly squeezed out). Cook until it leaves the sides of the fryer, stirring occasionally. If too dry add a little soup stock. Remove from the fire, put in a bowl, season with salt, pepper, ginger, and finely chopped parsley, add a small lump of fat, break in one whole egg, mix well and fill the fowl with it.

MEAT DRESSING FOR POULTRY

If you cannot buy sausage meat at your butcher's have him chop some for you, adding a little fat. Also mix in some veal with the beef while chopping. Season with salt, pepper, nutmeg or thyme. Grate in a piece of celery root and a piece of garlic about the size of a bean, add a small onion, a minced tomato, a quarter of a loaf of stale bread; also grated, and mix up the whole with one egg. If you prefer, you may soak the bread, press out every drop of water and dry in a heated spider with fat.

POTATO STUFFING

Add two cups of hot, mashed Irish or sweet potatoes to bread stuffing. Mix well and stuff in goose, stuffed veal or lamb breast, or in beef casings, cleaned and dressed.

CHESTNUT STUFFING

Shell and blanch two cups of chestnuts. Cook in boiling salted water until tender. Drain and force through a colander or a potato ricer. Add one-fourth cup of melted chicken fat, one-fourth teaspoon of pepper, three-fourths of a teaspoon of salt, one cup of grated bread crumbs, and enough soup stock to moisten.

RAISIN STUFFING

Take three cups of stale bread crumbs; add one-half a cup of melted chicken fat, one cup of seeded raisins cut in small pieces, one teaspoon of salt and one-fourth teaspoon of white pepper. Mix thoroughly.